GRAMMAR ESSENTIALS

Judith F. Olson

LEARNINGEXPRESS
NEW YORK

Copyright © 1997 Learning Express, LLC.

All rights reserved under International and Pan-American Copyright Conventions.
Published in the United States by LearningExpress, LLC, New York.

Library of Congress Cataloging-in-Publication Data

Olson, Judith F.
Grammar essentials / Judith F. Olson.—1st ed.
    p.   cm.—(Basics made easy)
    Includes index.
    ISBN 1-57685-062-5
    1. English Language—Grammar—Handbooks, manuals, ect. I. Title. II. Series.
PE1112.043   1997
428.2—dc21   97-4361
                                    CIP

Printed in the United States of America
9 8 7 6 5 4 3 2 1
First Edition

For Further Information
For information on LearningExpress, other LearningExpress products, or bulk sales,
please call or write to us at:
    LearningExpress®
    900 Broadway
    Suite 604
    New York, NY 10003
    212-995-2566

LearningExpress is an affiliated company of Random House, Inc.

Distributed to the retail trade by Random House, Inc., as agent for LearningExpress, LLC
Visit LearningExpress on the World Wide Web at www.learnx.com

ISBN 1-57685-062-5

7 85555 85062 0

CONTENTS

INTRODUCTION
HOW TO USE THIS BOOK

Writing is a lot like playing the piano. Some people enjoy it more than others, and people who are good at it study and practice it. No one is born playing the piano, but everyone can do it if they want. The same goes for writing. If you're interested in learning about writing and in becoming a better writer, this book will help you acquire the mysterious and coveted power of the pen.

This book covers the basics of writing: punctuation, usage, and diction. There's no fluff here; this book is for busy people who want to learn as much as they can as efficiently as possible. In 20 chapters, each of which you can complete in 20 minutes, you can improve your grasp of grammar. Each chapter contains lots of examples that illustrate the grammatical rules, and plenty of opportunities for you to practice the skills.

Many people are afraid of writing. They look at a blank sheet of paper or an empty computer screen and say, "I just don't know what to write. Even when I know what I want to say, I'm afraid it will come out looking wrong and sounding stupid."

But writing has three distinct advantage over speaking.

- **You can take it back.** Although writing is not instant communication and it doesn't not allow for immediate response and exchange, written communication can be retracted. Once words are spoken, you can never unspeak them. However, writing can be revised often until you've written the exact words in the exact tone you want. It's a more careful, thoughtful way of communicating.
- **You can make it clear.** The second advantage is that writing forces you to clarify your thoughts. If you're having trouble writing, it's usually because you're not yet finished with the thinking part. Sometimes just sitting down and writing whatever is on your mind helps you discover and organize what you think.
- **It lasts.** Another advantage is permanence. Ideas presented in writing carry far more weight than spoken ideas. Additionally, these ideas can be reviewed and referred to in their exact, original form. Spoken ideas rely upon the sometimes inaccurate memories of other people.

Writing is nothing more than thought on paper—considered, thoughtful thought. Many great ideas and observations are never born because their creators won't express them. You may have some wonderful things stuck inside your head with no way to get them out where others can see them. This book can help you express your ideas.

Develop your own plan for completing the 20 chapters in this book. They're designed to be completed in 20 minutes a day, but you may want to take more or less time with each lesson—or more time with chapters you find difficult and less with those you know cold. You could do a chapter each weekday and come out with a better knowledge of grammar in only a month. Or you may want to do more or fewer chapters at a time. You should, however, plan to complete at least two chapters a week. If you leave too much time between lessons, you'll forget what you've learned.

By the time you finish this book, you'll have much more confidence in your writing, and you'll probably be a better thinker. If you practice what you've learned, it won't take long for other people to notice the new and improved you.

CHAPTER | 1

Sometimes the words we use when we speak aren't effective when we write. This chapter discusses the difference between spoken and written English, informal language, wordiness, and precise language.

THE RIGHT WAY TO WRITE

Written language makes a permanent impression, one that can't be changed by rephrasing the words the way you can in a conversation. That's why it's important to write carefully. Take a look at the note below. What kind of an impression will it make?

Manny,

Got your note today. Thought I'd get right back to you. Keep you from getting in a tizzy about this whole moving thing. It's still kinda early to pack stuff for the move cause the new building isn't even done yet. Might as well wait til it is.

Seems like Jack has been chosen by the top dogs to head up the entire moving process with all its various aspects. Due to the fact that he hasn't started doing a thing yet, there's no sense in the rest of us getting our shorts in a wad about it. Don't freak out; it'll get done.

J.C.

SPOKEN ENGLISH VS. WRITTEN ENGLISH

Many of the speaking patterns we use are not suitable in business writing. For example, if you listen to a conversation you might hear incomplete sentences, sudden subject changes, or abbreviated versions of words and phrases. Although these may work fine in casual conversation, they are confusing and inappropriate when you are writing to a customer, supervisor, or employer. Avoid these things in written communication.

INCOMPLETE SENTENCES

Quite often we speak in thought fragments. We count on our tone of voice and our expression or the reaction of the listener to fill in the spaces. In writing this isn't possible, so it's important to write complete sentences that express complete thoughts. See Chapter 3 to learn how to avoid sentence fragments.

SUDDEN SUBJECT CHANGES

In everyday conversation we switch subjects easily. Two speakers can exchange far more information in two minutes than a reader can absorb in the same time period. That's why it's important to use the reader's time efficiently. Switching subjects requires time and mental energy. Write everything you have to say about one subject before moving on to the next. Link subjects together to make it easier for a reader to go from one idea to another. See Chapter 15 on making subjects agree with verbs.

ABBREVIATED WORDS

Many words we use in conversation are not used when we write. On the next page is a list of words frequently used in speech; however, the written versions are different.

Spoken Version	Written Version
cause, cuz	because
coulda	could have
gonna	going to
hafta	have to
kinda	kind of
shoulda	should have
sorta	sort of
till	until
wanna	want to
woulda	would have

SYMBOLS INSTEAD OF WORDS

Don't use symbols in place of words, even if it seems simpler or more efficient. Write out the complete word in any written communication if you want to be taken seriously.

> four (not *4*)
> to, too, two (not *2*)
> and (not *&*)
> extra (not *x-tra*)

COLLOQUIALISMS

Colloquialisms are informal words and phrases such as *in a bind, pulled it off, real good,* etc. These words and phrases are widely used in conversations between friends, but in business writing they portray an attitude of chumminess or close friendship that may cause your message to be taken less seriously than you intended or that may even insult your reader. A friendly, colloquial tone is fine in a personal letter; however, a more formal tone is better for business communications meant to be taken seriously. Compare the following paragraphs. If you received these two memos from your employees, which would you take more seriously?

> We're really in a bind on our end. Seems like every time we turn around something else comes up. Today was one of those days. A few of the guys who decided to live it up last

night couldn't get over it this morning. Since we were short-handed, we didn't come close to our daily quota. This is really ticking me off.

We're having trouble meeting our quota. New problems keep arising. Today was a difficult day. Several employees who stayed out late last night were unable to come to work on time. Because we were shorthanded, we missed our quota. This makes me angry.

The following sets of sentences illustrate the difference between colloquial and standard diction. The colloquial sentences in the first column are rewritten in the second column using more standard language.

Colloquial	Standard
The car works real good.	The car works **well**.
Ben got sick of waiting.	Ben **tired** of waiting.
I'm awful thirsty.	I'm **very** (or **quite** or **extremely**) thirsty.
It looks like they'll be late.	It looks **as if** (or **as though**) they'll be late.
The cake was real good.	The cake was **very** (or **quite**) good.
We're in a bind.	We're in **trouble**.
Drew put it off till tomorrow.	Drew **postponed** it until tomorrow.
I don't have that much of a chance.	I don't have **a very good** chance.
Rosa got there in time.	Rosa **arrived** in time.
Jill got the order.	Jill **received** the order.
I like to pal around with her.	I like to **spend time** with her.
Kip put across the wrong idea.	Kip **conveyed** the wrong idea.
I just don't get it.	I just don't **understand**.
How come you're leaving?	**Why** are you leaving?
What for?	**Why**?
I see where you're coming from.	I **understand your point**.
Leah had one of those days.	Leah had a **difficult** day.
Rodney can't make up his mind.	Rodney can't **decide**.
Robin will keep an eye on things.	Robin will **watch** things.
They're going to live it up tonight.	They're going to **celebrate** tonight.
The Knicks pulled it off.	The Knicks **succeeded**.

WORDINESS

Extra words waste space and time. Not only that, but they may also distort the message or make it difficult to understand. Get in the habit of streamlining your writing, making your sentences as concise as possible. If you use five words where three would do, delete the extra words or structure your sentences to avoid them. Look at the following examples.

Wordy: It was a twenty-minute period of time after the accident had occurred when the emergency vehicles arrived to lend assistance. [21 words]

Revised: The emergency vehicles arrived twenty minutes after the accident. [9 words]

Wordy: It was decided that the club would organize a committee for the purpose of conducting a search for a new leader. [21 words]

Revised: The club organized a committee to search for a new leader. [11 words]

The additional words add no information. All they do is take up space.

BUZZWORDS AND FLUFF

Buzzwords are words that sound important but don't add much meaning to writing. They include words such as *aspect, element, factor, scope, situation, type, kind,* and *forms.* Fluff words such as *absolutely, definitely, really, very, important, significant, current, major, quite,* etc., also may add length to a sentence, but like buzzwords, they seldom add meaning.

Wordy: The nature of the scheduling system is a very important matter that can definitely have a really significant impact on the morale aspect of an employee's attitude. Aspects of our current scheduling policy make it absolutely necessary that we undergo a significant change.

Revised: The scheduling system can affect employee morale. Our policy needs to be changed.

WORDY PHRASES

The following table lists a host of phrases that can be reduced to one or two words.

Wordy	Concise
puzzling in nature	puzzling
of a peculiar kind	peculiar
at this point in time	now, today
at that point in time	then
regardless of the fact that	although
due to the fact that	because
in order to	to
by means of	by
of an indefinite nature	indefinite
exhibits a tendency to	tends to
concerning the matter of	about
in connection with	with
in the event that	if
in relation to	with

Some wordiness is caused by passive voice. In **active voice,** the subject of a sentence is the source of the action in the sentence. In **passive voice,** the subject is acted on.

Passive: It has been decided that your application for promotion is not in line with the principles set up by the committee in the promotion application guidelines.
Active: The committee denied your promotion because it did not follow the application guidelines.

Passive: The letter of application was rejected by the board of governors.
Active: The board of governors rejected the application.

Writers sometimes stretch their sentences by using unnecessary words. The following table illustrates stretched sentences rewritten to be more concise.

Stretched Sentence	Concise Sentence
Alex seems to be impatient.	Alex seems impatient
We must know what it is that we are doing.	We must know what we're doing.
The reason we were late was because of traffic.	Traffic made us late.
These requests will be considered by us on an individual basis.	We'll consider these requests individually.
The musicians, who were distressed, left the hall.	The distressed musicians left the hall.
There are new problems arising daily.	New problems arise daily.
Due to the fact that we were early, we found great seats.	We came early and found great seats.
The consideration given in the latest evaluation is an example of how I was treated unfairly.	My last evaluation was not fair.

PRECISE LANGUAGE

Work to make your writing as precise as possible. In doing so, you will communicate more meaning while using fewer words. In other words, you will make your writing more concise. Choose words to help you transmit an exact meaning.

Imprecise	Precise
Homer managed the project.	Homer organized the staff and monitored progress.
Melody doesn't handle people well.	Melody yells at and insults coworkers.
Richard can relate to Patty.	Richard understands Patty's position.
This is a good proposal.	This proposal explains the problem and suggests a solution.
These bad instructions confused me.	These disorganized, vague instructions left me with no idea how to fix the stool.
We had a nice time with you.	We enjoyed eating your food, drinking your wine, and swimming in your pool.
I always have trouble with this machine.	I can never get this truck started.
I like to have fun at the company picnic.	I like to eat, visit, and play games at the company picnic.
We need to clean up before we go.	We need to put away the supplies and shower before we go.

Review

Remember the memo at the beginning of this chapter? Look at it again. Try to rewrite it by revising colloquial and informal language, eliminating wordiness, and using precise language. You can do this in many ways. Then turn back to this page and read the memo below as an example of one way of rewriting it.

Dear Manny,

I'm replying to your note about packing to move to the new building. Jack is organizing the packing and moving. Since the building is not yet finished, he hasn't started the process yet. I'm sure that if we're patient, everything will turn out fine. Don't worry. I'll let you know as soon as Jack begins work on the move.

J.C

CHAPTER | 2

This chapter teaches you about the basic unit of communication in the English language: the sentence. Mastering this chapter will give you the key to mastering everything else in this book—and your writing!

WHAT *IS* A SENTENCE, ANYWAY?

A sentence is the basic unit of thought in the English language. This chapter will help you learn to write a complete, coherent sentence.

THE PARTS OF A SENTENCE

A sentence has both a subject and a predicate and expresses a complete thought.

The snow is falling.

This is a sentence because it names what the sentence is talking about (snow) and tells us something about the snow (that it is falling). It also expresses a complete thought.

THE SUBJECT

The part of the sentence that tells us what the sentence is about is called the **subject**. The subject can be one word or several words. The **complete subject** consists of all the words that go together to make up the subject. The complete subjects are highlighted in each of the following sentences.

> **A loud argument** broke out at the game.
>
> **The worried, young pilot** read the storm warning.
>
> **The newspaper article** mentioned our newest menu item.

Every complete subject contains a **simple subject.** The simple subject, which is a noun or pronoun, is the most important word in the complete subject. It is the word that names what the sentence is about. Look at the complete subjects highlighted in the sentences above. Which word is the most important in each complete subject? The simple subject is highlighted below.

> A loud **argument**
>
> The worried, young **pilot**
>
> The newspaper **article**

Practice

Read the following sentences. In each one, identify the complete subject. Then underline the simple subject, or the main word that tells what the sentence is about. At the end of the chapter you will find the complete subjects, with the simple subjects highlighted.

1. My severe stomachache seemed better at the doctor's office.
2. Our new mail carrier slipped on the ice this morning.
3. The longest, dreariest road lies between the Nebraska borders.

THE PREDICATE

The part of the sentence that explains something about the subject is called the predicate. The predicate can be one word or several words. The **complete predicate** consists of all the words that go together to make up the predicate. The complete predicates are highlighted in each of the following sentences.

A loud argument **broke out at the game.**

The worried, young pilot **read the storm warning.**

The newspaper article **mentioned our newest menu item.**

Mrs. Dawson **is our most difficult customer.**

My neighbor **rarely complains about snow.**

Every complete predicate contains a **simple predicate,** or verb. The simple predicate is the word that shows action or helps to make a statement about the subject. Look at the complete predicates highlighted in the sentences above. Which word shows action or helps to make the statement about the subject? The simple predicates are highlighted below.

broke out at the game.

read the storm warning.

mentioned our newest menu item.

is our most difficult customer.

rarely **complains** about snow.

Practice

Read the following sentences. In each one, identify the complete predicate. Then underline the simple predicate, or the word that shows action or helps to make a statement about the subject. At the end of the chapter you will find the complete predicates, with the simple predicates highlighted.

4. The purple curtain ripped at the seams.

5. Our president always buys some of our competitor's products.

6. Dotted print backgrounds are difficult to read.

COMPOUND SUBJECTS AND PREDICATES

A sentence can have more than one subject joined by *and, or,* or *nor* and sharing the same verb. This is called a **compound subject.** The compound subjects are highlighted in the examples below.

Horace and **Beth** both asked for a promotion.

Hannah and **Terri** are the shift supervisors in this department.

A sentence can also have a **compound predicate:** more than one predicate joined by *and, or,* or *nor.*

> Dimitri **wrote** a letter and **sent** it to the personnel department.
>
> Horace **called** his supervisor and **asked** for a meeting.

CLAUSES

Like sentences, **clauses** are groups of words that have a subject and a predicate. Clauses are either **independent** or **dependent**.

INDEPENDENT CLAUSES

Independent clauses are groups of words in a sentence that can stand alone, because they express a complete thought. The **simple sentence** consists of one independent clause:

> The snow is falling.

Sometimes more than one independent clause is included in the same sentence, which is known as a **compound sentence.** When this happens, the clauses are separated by a comma and a **conjunction**, or joining word (*and, but, or, for, nor, so, yet*). The independent clauses are underlined in the following sentences.

> A wasp stung me, and I had to go to the hospital for treatment.
> The door was open, but I was afraid to walk inside.
> We need to drive a little faster, or we need to get an earlier start.

DEPENDENT CLAUSES

Dependent clauses, also known as subordinate clauses, are groups of words in a sentence that have a subject and predicate but can't stand alone because they don't express a complete thought:

> When I saw the snow was falling

Sometimes sentences are made up of one independent clause and one or more dependent clauses. These are known as **complex sentences.** In the following sentence, the independent clause is highlighted and the dependent clause is underlined.

> **I put on my heavy coat** when I saw the snow was falling.

Practice

Underline the independent clauses in the sentences below. Check your work with the answers at the end of the chapter.

   7. Believing that the pages were in the right order, I mailed the manuscript.

   8. I wanted to renew the lease before the end of the year, because I liked the house.

   9. Whenever the weather forecasters predict rain, the sun shines.

  10. In the box sitting underneath the desk, I found my hat.

  11. I called Tom again, and the new programs finally arrived.

  12. I went for a walk today, and I mailed your letter.

Answers

   1. My severe **stomachache**

   2. Our new mail **carrier**

   3. The longest, dreariest **road**

   4. **ripped** at the seams.

   5. always **buys** some of our competitor's products.

   6. **are** difficult to read.

   7. Believing that the pages were in the right order, <u>I mailed the manuscript.</u>

   8. <u>I wanted to renew the lease before the end of the year</u>, because I liked the house.

   9. Whenever the weather forecasters predict rain, <u>the sun shines.</u>

  10. In the box sitting underneath the desk, <u>I found my hat.</u>

  11. <u>I called Tom again</u>, and <u>the new programs finally arrived.</u>

  12. <u>I went for a walk today</u>, and <u>I mailed your letter.</u>

CHAPTER | 3

Don't stop. Before the sentence is done. Sentence fragments—incomplete sentences—are popular with advertisers, but they have no place in your writing for work or school. By the time you finish this chapter, you'll be able to recognize and correct incomplete sentences in your writing.

FILLING OUT SENTENCE FRAGMENTS

In the English language, we write in complete sentences because they best communicate our ideas accurately. A well-written sentence leaves little room for the reader to misunderstand. The memo you see here is nearly impossible to understand because the writer uses incomplete sentences, or **sentence fragments,** rather than complete sentences. Bob has no idea what Bart needs.

> Bob,
> Can't get this to work. Think it's got something wrong with the alternator. Been a problem already. You remember. Can you fix this? Need it before the convention next week.
>
> Bart

Review

In the last chapter you learned that independent clauses are parts of sentences that can stand alone, while dependent clauses are parts of sentences that can't stand alone because they do not express a complete thought. Sometimes dependent clauses are used in the place of complete sentences. When this happens, they are considered sentence fragments. Any group of words that is punctuated as a sentence but that does not express a complete thought is called a **sentence fragment.**

DEPENDENT CLAUSES AS SENTENCE FRAGMENTS

A dependent, or subordinate, clause cannot stand by itself as a sentence; it needs an independent clause to support it. Look at the following groups of words. Even though they contain a subject and a verb, their meaning is incomplete. The subject in each dependent clause is highlighted, and the verb is underlined.

Before **we** went on to the next project

Whenever this **company** changes its policies

If the **road** is too icy for traffic

Look carefully at the following examples. They illustrate the difference between an independent clause and a dependent clause. The subjects are highlighted and the verbs are underlined in each example.

I left an hour later than normal. (Independent clause: sentence)

If **I** left an hour later than normal (Dependent clause: fragment)

When our **group** finished its report (Subordinate clause: fragment)

Our **group** finished its report. (Independent clause: sentence)

Whenever **Rita** tried to explain herself (Subordinate clause: fragment)

Rita tried to explain herself. (Independent clause: sentence)

SUBORDINATE CONJUNCTIONS

Look carefully at the examples above. Each dependent clause is longer than the independent clause. The groups of words are the same, but the dependent clauses have an extra word at the beginning. These words are called **subordinate conjunctions,** because they modify a dependent, or subordinate, clause in some way.

If a group of words that would normally be a complete sentence is preceded by a subordinate conjunction, something more is needed to complete the thought. In the sentences below, each of those fragments has been rewritten to express a complete thought. Notice that each sentence now has both an independent and a dependent clause. The dependent clauses are highlighted and the independent clauses are underlined in each clause.

> **If I left an hour later than normal,** <u>I missed my favorite talk show.</u>
> **When our group finished its report,** <u>we left for lunch.</u>
> **Whenever Rita tried to explain herself,** <u>she confused her words.</u>

Here is a list of some of the words that can be used as subordinate conjunctions:

after	*if*	*though*	*where*
although	*once*	*unless*	*wherever*
as	*since*	*until*	*while*
because	*than*	*when*	
before	*that*	*whenever*	

Sometimes a subordinate conjunction is a phrase rather than a single word:

> **as if** the storm had never happened
> **as though** we had always known
> **as long as** he can figure this out
> **as soon as** she understands the difference
> **even though** we are leaving
> **in order that** all of us can share in the work
> **so that** no one does more than his/her share

Make complete sentences out of the following fragments by adding an independent clause to each subordinate clause.

> Unless the highway commission buys the property,
> As long as Estelle is in charge,
> If we ever need help,

PHRASES AS SENTENCE FRAGMENTS

Dependent clauses are only one type of sentence fragment. Look at the word groups below. In each pair choose the group of words that expresses a complete thought. The other group of words in each pair is a fragment. See if you notice any similarities among the groups of words that are fragments.

The class was ready for the next step.
Talking to the owner.

Watching the sky.
The picnickers saw the air show.

Alone for the first time in years.
I comforted my grandmother.

Emily sat on the sofa.
Wondering what to do next.

These fragments are made up of **phrases:** groups of word that do not contain a subject or a predicate and do not complete a thought. Combining the two sets of words in each pair will make one complete sentence. With some of the word pairs, only a comma is needed. With others, a few extra words must be added to incorporate the phrase into the rest of the sentence. The examples below demonstrate how this is done.

The class was ready for the next step, talking to the owner.
Watching the sky, the picnickers saw the air show.
Since she was alone for the first time in years, I comforted my grandmother.
Emily sat on the sofa, wondering what to do next.

Practice

Combine the following word pairs into a complete sentence. Check your work with the corrected sentences at the end of the chapter. Often, there is more than one way to combine the word groups.

1. The next train will be arriving. Soon after the last one.
2. Not liking it one bit. Jane ate the casserole.
3. They used a fog machine to create the effect of smoke. One from an Army surplus store.

4. Send your news on letterhead stationary. Representing your company.

5. Not long before the last witness had testified. The judge ran out of patience.

SEPARATED FRAGMENTS

Sometimes a fragment is part of a complete sentence, but it is written as a separate sentence. Look at each of the word groups below. In each pair, one is a complete sentence; the other is a fragment. See if you can figure out which word group expresses a complete thought.

The fans drove all over the downtown area.
And looked for a parking spot.

And noticed an old classmate in the crowd scene.
We saw the movie.

Faulty equipment and poor workmanship.
They refused to pay the bill in full.

In the pond outside our building.
Canada geese have built a nest.

The set of words highlighted below represent a complete sentence. Combining the two sets of words in each pair makes both sets part of a complete sentence. Try combining the examples yourself.

The fans drove all over the downtown area.
And looked for a parking spot.

And noticed an old classmate in the crowd scene.
We saw the movie.

Faulty equipment and poor workmanship.
They refused to pay the bill in full.

In the pond outside our building.
Canada geese have built a nest.

Combined Sentences

There's more than one way to combine the sentences, but here's one.

> The fans drove all over the downtown area and looked for a parking spot.
>
> We saw the movie and noticed an old classmate in the crowd scene.
>
> They refused to pay the bill because of faulty equipment and poor workmanship.
>
> In the pond outside our building, Canadian geese have built a nest.

Review

Read each of the following word groups. If the word group is a sentence, identify the subject(s) and the verb(s). If the word group is a fragment, think of a way to make it into a complete sentence. Check your work with the answers at the end of the chapter. Those that are fragments have been rewritten. Keep in mind that there are many ways to correct a fragment. Only one is printed. If the word group is a sentence, the subjects have been highlighted and the verbs underlined in the answer.

6. Wishing he were almost anywhere else.
7. In the end, it made no difference at all.
8. That camping outside would be fun.
9. Before the part stops working altogether.
10. The unidentified man looked like a reporter.

Go back to Bart's memo at the beginning of the chapter. Here are the facts concerning Bart's situation.

- Bart is part of the grounds crew for a convention center.
- Bart regularly uses a riding lawn mower.
- The mower broke down three weeks ago.
- Bob sent the mower to be fixed.
- The alternator was replaced with a rebuilt one.
- The biggest event of the year is scheduled to begin in eight days.
- The grounds need to look "perfect."
- Bart needs a working mower to do his job.
- The mower will not start.
- When it is jump-started, the battery does not charge.

Try rewriting Bart's memo. Compare your version to the one below.

> Bob,
>
> The riding lawn mower we put a rebuilt alternator into three weeks ago isn't starting. When we jump-start it, the battery doesn't charge. I think the alternator is broken again. We need this fixed right away if we're going to be ready for the convention next week. Would you please see that the mower gets fixed? Thank you.
>
> Bart

Answers

1. The next train will be arriving soon after the last one.
   Soon after the last one, the next train will be arriving.
2. Not liking it one bit, Jane ate the casserole.
   Jane ate the casserole, not liking it one bit.
3. They used a fog machine from an Army surplus store to create the effect of smoke.
4. Send your news on letterhead stationary representing your company.
5. The judge ran out of patience not long before the last witness had testified.
   Not long before the last witness had testified, the judge ran out of patience.
6. Wishing he were almost anywhere else, Steve moaned and hung his head.
7. **Sentence**. In the end, **it** <u>made</u> no difference at all.
8. The Kern family thought that camping outside would be fun.
9. Before the part stops working altogether, we should order a replacement.
10. **Sentence**. The unidentified **man** <u>looked</u> like a reporter.

CHAPTER | 4

This chapter explains how to spot two problems that can keep people from understanding what you write: run-on sentences and comma splices. This chapter shows you how to correct and avoid both of these problems.

PUTTING A STOP TO GOING ON AND ON

Have you heard any of the radio or TV advertisements that use speed speakers, those people who can utter four or five sentences in five seconds? What they say is difficult to understand because there is no break in the sound. A listener has a hard time picking up what they say. The same thing can happen in writing. Read the following memo. Although you can probably understand what it says, doing so will not be easy. In fact, you may need to read the memo several times to figure out the meaning.

To: Arlis Schaffer
From: Gerald Lentz
Re: New floor buffer
Date: March 5, 1997

The buffer we got last week from Holton Supply has a few problems it doesn't always start when you flip the switch and it seems a little hesitant like it loses power every once in a while when I'm running it also the pads that came with it don't fit exactly right they are about an inch too small when the machine runs the outside part of it is not covered and often scratches the floor that's not good because it takes me forever to work out the scratches that the machine is supposed to avoid making instead of saving me time this machine is costing me more time. We need someone to look at the switch and we need to order the right size pads and it wouldn't hurt to see if they can find anything else wrong with this machine I just don't trust it.

This memo is hard to understand because some of the sentences run on without a break. We call these sentence run-ons. This chapter shows you how to avoid and correct run-on sentences when you write.

RUN-ON SENTENCES

As you know, an independent clause is a group of words that could be a complete sentence all by itself. In a **run-on sentence**, independent clauses are run together as one sentence without being separated by any punctuation (a period, semicolon, or comma).

The best way to avoid run-on sentences is to write simple sentences, each explaining one thought. When you finish explaining one thought, end the sentence. Your sentences will be very short, but they will also be easy to understand.

Sayjo bused the dishes.
Nicole stacked them in the dishwasher.
Amber unloaded the dishwasher.
Chris restocked the shelves.

Quite often, more than one idea must be presented in a sentence. As discussed in Chapter 2, this kind of sentence, which is called a compound sentence, is made up of two or more independent clauses. When written correctly, the clauses are separated by words and/or punctuation. The sentences below contain more than one independent clause, but the clauses have been run together without words or punctuation. This makes them run-on sentences.

> Alan left the city he couldn't stand all the buildings.
> This year's vacation seemed short it lasted only a week.
> We stopped for lunch we were starving.

All three of these examples can be corrected quite easily in one of four ways.

1. By adding a period and a capital letter, making two simple sentences.
   > Alan left the city. He couldn't stand all the buildings.
   > This year's vacation seemed short. It lasted only a week.
   > We stopped for lunch. We were starving.

2. By adding a comma and a conjunction (*and, but, or, for, nor, yet, so*).
   > Alan couldn't stand all the buildings, and he left the city.
   >> (Notice that the clauses have been reversed.)
   > This year's vacation seemed short, and it lasted only a week.
   > We were starving, so we stopped for lunch.

3. By adding a semicolon.
   > Alan left the city; he couldn't stand the buildings.
   > This year's vacation seemed short; it lasted only a week.
   > We stopped for lunch; we were starving.

4. By turning one of the two independent clauses into a dependent clause. To do this, you need to add a subordinate conjunction where it fits in the sentence and reword the sentence if necessary. Remember the list of subordinate conjunctions from the last chapter?
   > **Because** Alan couldn't stand all the buildings, he left the city.
   > Alan left the city **because** he couldn't stand all the buildings.

   > **Since** it lasted only a week, this year's vacation seemed short.
   > This year's vacation seemed short **since** it lasted only a week.

25

Since we were starving, we stopped for lunch.

We stopped for lunch **because** we were starving.

In these examples, all three sentences have been rewritten in two ways: by putting the dependent clause at the beginning of the sentence, and by putting it at the end. Notice how the comma is used in each pair of examples. If the dependent clause comes first, it is set off by a comma. No comma is needed if the dependent clause follows the independent clause.

Practice

Look at each of the run-on sentences below. Correct them so they are no longer run-on. Check your work with the answers at the end of the chapter.

1. The personnel director gave us bonus checks the president shook our hands.
2. Evelyn signed the work order she gave it to the secretary.
3. Sam listens to music when he works it relaxes him.
4. Barry took the short cut he ended up lost.
5. My sweatshirt was ruined I spilled acid on it.

COMMA SPLICES

Another kind of problem sentence, called a comma splice, is unclear for the reader because only a comma is used to separate two independent clauses.

Mr. Klein is bald, his wife has long frizzy hair.

Jacob did the raking, Matthew did the mowing.

Weldon bought the groceries, Nancy cooked dinner.

In a compound sentence, independent clauses must be separated in one of two ways:

1. Separate independent clauses with a comma and a conjunction (*and, but, so, or, for, nor, yet*).

    Mr. Klein is bald, but his wife has long frizzy hair.

    Jacob did the raking, and Matthew did the mowing.

    Weldon bought the groceries, so Nancy cooked dinner.

2. Separate independent clauses with a semicolon.

    Mr. Klein is bald; his wife has long frizzy hair.

    Jacob did the raking; Matthew did the mowing.

    Weldon bought the groceries; Nancy cooked dinner.

Practice

Look at each of the comma splices below. Correct them so that each is still one sentence but is written correctly. Check your work with the answers at the end of the chapter.

    6. Henry lives across the street, he has been there for twenty-five years.

    7. Mary heads the search committee, John is the recorder.

    8. Sid gave demonstrations all summer long, he returned in the fall.

    9. Mary posted the work schedule, Peter requested a change.

    10. Kent brought the problem to our attention, we fixed it immediately.

CONJUNCTIVE ADVERBS

Some run-on sentences and commas splices happen because people use words like *however, therefore,* and *then* as if they were conjunctions.

> I wanted a new sports car however my bank account wouldn't support one.

> My sister Dorothy thought she was cheated, therefore, she wanted her money back.

> We stopped for lunch then we got back to work.

Unlike conjunctions, which simply join words together, words such as *however, therefore,* and *then* are a special kind of adverb that expresses a relationship between clauses. This kind of adverb, called a *conjunctive adverb,* cannot join two independent clauses the way a conjunction does.

To correct this kind of commas splice or run-on, make two sentences, or put a semicolon between the two main clauses and set the adverb off from the rest of the clause with a comma. Note that you can move the adverb around in its clause without changing the meaning—which is how you can tell the difference between this kind of adverb and a subordinate conjunction. You can move *however* around in its clause, but you can't move *because* around in its clause.

> I wanted a new sports car. However, my bank account wouldn't support one.

> I wanted a new sports car; however, my bank account wouldn't support one.

> I wanted a new sports car; my bank account, however, wouldn't support one.

My sister Dorothy thought she was cheated. She therefore wanted
her money back.

My sister Dorothy thought she was cheated; therefore, she wanted
her money back.

My sister Dorothy thought she was cheated; she therefore wanted
her money back

We stopped for lunch. Then we got back to work.

We stopped for lunch; then we got back to work.

We stopped for lunch. We then got back to work.

Practice

Use what you have learned about commas and semicolons to correct the
following sentences. Check your work with the answers at the end of the
chapter.

11. These microscope cases are falling apart the lenses of these microscopes however are very durable.

12. Maribeth's coat was in the cloakroom however she had left an hour
ago.

13. A drug test is not required for this job the central office will need
your fingerprints however.

Remember the memo from the beginning of the chapter? Go back to it
and correct the run-on sentences. Compare your version with the one
printed here.

To: Arlis Schaffer
From: Gerald Lentz
Re: New floor buffer
Date: March 5, 1997

The buffer we got last week from Holton Supply has a few
problems. It doesn't always start up when you flip the switch,
and it seems a little hesitant. It loses power every once in a
while when I'm running it. Also the pads that came with it
don't fit exactly right. They are about an inch too small.
When the machine runs, the outside part of it is not covered,

so it often scratches the floor. That's not good because it takes me forever to work out the scratches that the machine is supposed to avoid making. Instead of saving me time, this machine is costing me more time. We need someone to look at the switch, and we need to order the right size pads. It wouldn't hurt to see if they can find anything else wrong with this machine. I just don't trust it.

Review

Use what you have learned about complete sentences, sentence fragments, run-ons, and comma splices. In each of the numbered items below, decide whether the group of words is a correctly written sentence or sentences. If it is not, rewrite it to make it correct. Check your version with the ones given at the end of the chapter.

14. Mr. France introduced me to the speaker. A neighbor of his.
15. Last night my supervisor called. To ask me if I could stay an extra three hours today.
16. I liked the new batch of chemicals, they kept mildew from forming on wet surfaces.
17. I looked in my mailbox. Hoping to find my paycheck.
18. I saw it. The key I had lost.
19. After I had read the entire manual.
20. Jeremy filled the order, it arrived at the warehouse around noon.
21. Ilya locked the doors we left the building.
22. Our surveillance system has cut down on shoplifting.
23. Lying on the floor next to the coffee table.

Answers

1. The personnel director gave us bonus checks. The president shook our hands.

   The personnel director gave us bonus checks, and the president shook our hands.

   The personnel director gave us bonus checks while the president shook our hands.

2. Evelyn signed the work order. She gave it to the secretary.

   Evelyn signed the work order, and she gave it to the secretary.

   Evelyn signed the work order before she gave it to the secretary.

3. Sam listens to music when he works. It relaxes him.

Sam listens to music when he works, and it relaxes him.

Sam listens to music when he works because it relaxes him.

4. Barry took the short cut. He ended up lost.

Barry took the short cut, and he ended up lost.

Because Barry took the short cut, he ended up lost.

5. My sweatshirt was ruined. I spilled acid on it.

I spilled acid on my sweatshirt, and it was ruined.

My sweatshirt was ruined because I spilled acid on it.

6. Henry lives across the street; he has been there for twenty-five years.

Henry lives across the street, and he has been there for twenty-five years.

7. Mary heads the search committee; John is the recorder.

Mary heads the search committee, and John is the recorder.

8. Sid gave demonstrations all summer long; he returned in the fall.

Sid gave demonstrations all summer long, and he returned in the fall.

9. Mary posted the work schedule; Peter requested a change.

Mary posted the work schedule, and Peter requested a change.

10. Kent brought the problem to our attention; we fixed it immediately.

Kent brought the problem to our attention, and we fixed it immediately.

11. These microscope cases are falling apart; the lenses of these microscopes, however, are very durable.

12. Maribeth's coat was in the cloakroom; however, she had left an hour ago.

13. A drug test is not required for this job; the central office will need your fingerprints, however.

14. Mr. France introduced me to the speaker, a neighbor of his.

15. Last night my supervisor called to ask me if I could stay an extra three hours today.

16. I liked the new batch of chemicals; they kept mildew from forming on wet surfaces.

I liked the new batch of chemicals because they kept mildew from forming on wet surfaces.

17. I looked in my mailbox, hoping to find my paycheck.

18. I saw it, the key I had lost.

19. After I had read the entire manual, I understood how to operate the equipment.

20. Jeremy filled the order. It arrived at the warehouse around noon.
Jeremy filled the order when it arrived at the warehouse around noon.

21. Ilya locked the doors. We left the building.
Ilya locked the doors, and we left the building.
Ilya locked the doors after we left the building.

22. Sentence

23. We found the lost catalog lying on the floor next to the coffee table.

CHAPTER | 5

Now that you know what a sentence is, it won't hurt to review how to begin and end a sentence. This chapter shows you how to use capital letters—not only those at the beginnings of sentences—and periods, question marks, and exclamation points.

GOOD BEGINNINGS, GOOD ENDINGS

Capital letters are good beginnings—not only for sentences, but also for a variety of kinds of words. Periods are good endings, both for most sentences and also for abbreviations and other uses. Then, too, question marks and exclamation points can provide a little spice in your writing. This chapter helps you master them all.

Read this memo from Mike:

I need a New router and a Band saw. Wards has them on sale this week. A skil saw would be nice sometimes one isn't enough since there are three of us who use it. Black and decker is also okay? If you want, I can pick them up at the store for you.

Mike

What exactly does Mike want? The first sentence makes it clear that he want a router and a saw. The rest of the memo leads to nothing but questions: Does he want a band saw made by Skil, or a circular saw (sometimes called a skill saw) by Band? This confusion comes up because Mike hasn't punctuated his memo properly or put capital letters where they belong.

CAPITAL LETTERS
GENERAL CAPITALIZATION RULES

Here are some rules for capitalization.

- Capitalize the first word of a sentence. If the first word is a number, write it as a word.

    That was a wonderful party.

    Five of us finished the project.

- Capital the pronoun I or any contraction made using *I (I'm, I'd, I've, I'll)*.

    The mail carrier stopped when **I** asked for help.

    My mother thought that **I'**d be home for Christmas.

    I know **I'**ll be finished by noon.

- Capitalize proper nouns, but not common nouns.

    A proper noun refers to a specific person, place, or thing. A common noun refers to a general class of people, places, or things. For example, *microwave* is a common noun. It is the general name for a kitchen appliance. However, Sharp is a proper noun because it names a specific kind of microwave. Proper nouns are capitalized; common nouns are not.

Proper Nouns	Common Nouns
Janice	aunt
Baton Rouge	city
Roosevelt High School	school
Buick	car
Walmart	store

- Capitalize the first word of a quotation.

  "When will you be finished?"

  "Good morning," said my new neighbor as I approached the door.

  "Good morning!" I answered, somewhat surprised. "You must be Sylvia."

- Do *not* capitalize the first word of a partial quotation.

  He called her "the best problem solver alive."

  "The new edition," Ari explained, "will be available in two months."

Practice

Check your knowledge of these rules with the sentences below. Circle the letters that should be capitalized in each sentence. Make a diagonal mark through the letters that are capitalized, but should not be. Check your work with the correct versions of sentences at the end of the chapter. The changes are highlighted for you.

1. the instructions were clear. after a careful reading, i could understand them completely.
2. "what do you think you're doing?" my Uncle jack asked.
3. "i'm putting together this gas grill," i answered.
4. the newspaper said our new owner was "An industrial visionary."
5. my new Car is an oldsmobile cutlass.

PROPER NOUNS

All proper nouns—words that name a specific person, place, or thing—must be capitalized. Remembering which nouns are proper can be difficult. The table below includes the most common categories of proper nouns.

Category of Proper Nouns	Example
days of the week	Sunday, Tuesday
months	March, April
holidays	Easter, Passover
historical events, periods, documents	Revolutionary War (event) Middle Ages (period) U.S. Constitution (document)
special events, calendar events	Sausage Festival Mother's Day Memorial Day
names of people and places	Steven Jones, Kennedy Center, World Trade Center
names of structures, buildings	Lincoln Memorial, Travelers Building
names of trains, ships, aircraft, other modes of transportation	Queen Elizabeth, Discovery, Northern Pacific, Vanguard Airlines
names of products	Dial soap, Jeep Cherokee
names of officials	Senator Kennedy, President Clinton
works of art and literature	*Tobacco Road* (book) "Harlem" (poem)
ethnic groups, races, languages, nationalities	Italian/American, Asian, German, Spanish
cities, states, and governmental units	Sioux City, Iowa; Anchorage, Alaska; Republic of China
streets, highways, and roads	Locust Avenue, Interstate 80, Havelin Boulevard
landmarks and geographical locations	Rocky Mountains, International Date Line
public areas and bodies of water	Chippewa Forest, Raccoon River
institutions, organizations and businesses	Luther College, Rotary Club, Bellwether Ford

Practice

Using the rules above, circle the letters that should be capitalized in each of the following sentences. Make a diagonal mark through any letters that are capitalized, but should not be. Check your work with the corrected versions of the sentences at the end of the chapter. The changes are high-lighted for you in the answers.

6. shakespeare was the most prolific author of the renaissance.
7. the nelsons spent thanksgiving Day with Relatives.
8. andy began work on thursday, april 3.
9. my Friend jon has two Nephews who fought in desert storm
10. Additional Security guards will be hired for the talking heads concert.
11. The convention group caught the amtrak in omaha.
12. Ling applied for admission to the university of Iowa.
13. In canada, some citizens speak french, and others speak english.
14. We followed the colorado river to the border of arizona.
15. Ammar works for apex construction company.

PROPER ADJECTIVES

An **adjective** is a word that describes or tells us more about a person, place, or thing. A proper adjective is derived from a proper noun. Many proper adjectives refer to a nationality. Most proper adjectives should be capitalized, such as *English muffin, Polish sausage, French customs.*

Practice

Circle the letters that should be capitalized in the following sentences. Check your work with the corrected versions of the sentences at the end of the chapter. The changes are highlighted for you.

16. Amasu prefers italian dressing on her salad.
17. When I win the lottery, I intend to buy a polynesian island.
18. We were delayed at the canadian border.

WHEN NOT TO CAPITALIZE

- Avoid unnecessarily capitalizing compass directions. However, direction words that refer to a specific area of the country should be capitalized. Direction words are not capitalized unless they specifically refer to a part of the country.

   We headed east to avoid the storm.

   The computer industry flourished in the West.

- Avoid unnecessarily capitalizing the words referring to family members. Capitalize them only when they are used as names.

   Although Aunt Matilda has arrived, my other aunts are late.

   After my mother lectured me, Father yelled.

   Look closely at the second example. If a word such as *my, our, your, his, her,* or *their* comes before the word referring to a family member, it is not capitalized. The word *mother* is not capitalized because the word *my* comes before it. However, no such word comes before *Father.* In fact, *Father* is used in place of the man's name, making it a proper name. That is why it is capitalized.

- Avoid unnecessarily capitalizing the seasons of the year or parts of the academic year.

   The university offers Basic Computing 405 in the spring semester.

   Marge plants her perennials in the early fall.

- Avoid unnecessarily capitalizing school subjects. They should be capitalized only if they are part of the name of a specific course.

   I try to avoid science courses because I'm squeamish.

   Nyrupama is taking Biology II next semester.

- Avoid unnecessarily capitalizing words modified by proper adjectives.

   Polish sausage, not Polish Sausage

   Italian restaurant, not Italian Restaurant

Practice

Using the rules above, circle the letters that should be capitalized in each of the following sentences. Make a diagonal mark through any letters that are capitalized but should not be. Check your work with the corrected versions of the sentences at the end of the chapter. The changes are highlighted for you.

19. The great plains are located in the midwest.
20. Cynthia turned West at the stop sign.
21. If my Cousin Kathy comes to the picnic, I know aunt Jan won't.
22. Jacob is an outstanding History student.
23. We went to a sri lankan Restaurant in minneapolis.

END PUNCTUATION
WHEN TO USE QUESTION MARKS

Use a question mark after a word or a group of words that asks a question.

> Where?
>
> Okay?
>
> What did you do last night?
>
> Will you cover the tomatoes so they don't freeze?

Sentences that begin with these words are usually questions:

who	*where*
what	*why*
when	*how*

WHEN TO USE PERIODS

- Use a period at the end of a sentence that makes a statement.

    > Many jobs require a working knowledge of computers.
    >
    > Thomas Jefferson is the most famous American slave owner.
    >
    > The tour bus leaves right after breakfast in the morning.

- Use a period at the end of sentence that makes a request, gives an instruction, or states a command.

    > Take this to the mailbox before you leave.
    >
    > Open the cover, remove item B, and close the box.
    >
    > Check the message board before you go home.

- Use a period at the end of a sentence that asks an indirect question.

    > Have you seen my coat? (direct question)
    >
    > My boss asked if I had seen her coat. (indirect question)
    >
    > How did you know what to do? (direct question)
    >
    > Hayden wanted to know how we knew what to do. (indirect question)
    >
    > Will you help me? (direct question)
    >
    > Rachel asked if I would help her. (indirect question)

Practice

Place a period or a question mark at the end of each of these sentences.
Check your work with the corrected versions of the sentences at the end
of the chapter.

24. Cyril asked me to find the new order that arrived today
25. Do you think we'll be finished by the end of the day
26. Today is colder than yesterday
27. When do you plan to order the supplies we need
28. Leave the packages on the counter by the window

OTHER USES FOR PERIODS

- Use a period (also called a decimal point) before a decimal.

    A gallon equals 3.875 liters.

    Only 5.6% of our employees chose vision care.

- Use a period between dollars and cents.

    The new paneling is $45.95 a sheet.

    Do you have $4.50 that I can borrow?

- Use a period after an initial in a personal name.

    The patient in room 202 is Ron P. Martel.

    The book was written by J. R. R. Tolkien.

    A. J. Foyt races cars.

- Use a period after an abbreviation.

    The plane leaves at 3:17 on Jan. 1.

    Smith Bros. is hiring subcontractors for this job.

    The apt. complex at the corner of Woodland Ave. and 1st St.
    belongs to me.

WHEN NOT TO USE PERIODS

- If an abbreviation comes at the end of a sentence, only one period
  is needed.

    We delivered the desk to Koch & Co.

    This trailer was machined at Dee Zee Inc.

    The box is 3 in. by 5 in.

- If an abbreviation has become a commonly used name for something, no period is needed.
  > gym (gymnasium)
  > exam (examination)
  > auto (automobile)

- If an abbreviation has become an acronym, or a name widely recognized by its initials (TV, WHO, FBI, NATO, NASA), no period is needed.
  > Velma is scheduled for an MRI at 3 o'clock this afternoon.
  > The Smiths mailed their tax forms to the IRS.
  > My niece works for the CIA.

Practice

Use what you know about periods to correct these sentences. Check your sentences with the corrected sentences at the end of the chapter.

29. The plane left Omaha, Neb, and arrived at Tampa Bay, Fla, at 2:23

30. Mr Drish and Dr P M Staplin left for the convention this morning

31. The patients' rooms measured 14 ft by 17 ft

32. I sold my used CD for $3 99

33. Go ahead Explain what you mean

WHEN TO USE EXCLAMATION POINTS

- Use an exclamation point after an outcry or sentence that expresses strong feeling.
  > Darn it!
  > Good grief!
  > Watch out for that truck!
  > I don't think I can take this anymore!

Warning! Exclamation points are a little bit like salt on food. Be careful not to overdo them.

- Use an exclamation point after an exclamation that begins with a question word (*who, what, when, where, why, how*) but doesn't ask a question.
  > How forgetful I am!
  > What a lot of trouble for such a small result!

Practice

Use what you know about questions marks, periods, and exclamation points to correct these sentences. Check your work with the corrected versions of the sentences at the end of the chapter.

34. Help! I can't breathe?
35. I got my income tax forms in the mail today!
36. Will you check this order for me.
37. Those plumbers? Do you know what they did!
38. I'm amazed at how quickly she moved?

Review

Remember the memo from Mike at the beginning of the chapter? He rewrote it using proper capitalization and endmarks. Now his supervisor knows exactly what he wants.

> I need a new router and a band saw. Sometimes one saw isn't enough since there are three of us who use it. A Skil saw would be nice. Black and Decker is also okay. Wards has them on sale this week. If you want, I can pick them up at the store for you.
>
> Mike

Answers

1. The instructions were clear. After a careful reading, I could understand them completely.
2. "What do you think you're doing?" my uncle Jack asked.
3. "I'm putting together this gas grill," I answered.
4. The newspaper said our new owner was "an industrial visionary."
5. My new car is an Oldsmobile Cutlass.
6. Shakespeare was the most prolific author of the Renaissance.
7. The Nelsons spent Thanksgiving Day with relatives.
8. Andy began work on Thursday, April 3.
9. My friend Jon has two nephews who fought in Desert Storm.
10. Additional security guards will be hired for the Talking Heads concert.
11. The convention group caught the Amtrak in Omaha.
12. Ling applied for admission to the University of Iowa.

13. In Canada, some citizens speak French, and others speak English.

14. We followed the Colorado River to the border of Arizona.

15. Ammar works for Apex Construction Company.

16. Amasu prefers Italian dressing on her salad.

17. When I win the lottery, I intend to buy a Polynesian island.

18. We were delayed at the Canadian border.

19. The Great Plains are located in the Midwest.

20. Cynthia turned west at the stop sign.

21. If my cousin Kathy comes to the picnic, I know Aunt Jan won't.

22. Jacob is an outstanding history student.

23. We went to a Sri Lankan restaurant in Minneapolis

24. Cyril asked me to find the new order that arrived today.

25. Do you think we'll be finished by the end of the day?

26. Today is colder than yesterday.

27. When do you plan to order the supplies we need?

28. Leave the packages on the counter by the window.

29. The plane left Omaha, Neb., and arrived at Tampa Bay, Fla., at 2:23.

30. Mr. Drish and Dr. P. M. Staplin left for the convention this morning.

31. The patients' rooms measured 14 ft. by 17 ft.

32. I sold my used CD for $3.99.

33. Go ahead. Explain what you mean.

34. Help! I can't breathe!

35. I got my income tax forms in the mail today.

36. Will you check this order for me?

37. Those plumbers! Do you know what they did?

38. I'm amazed at how quickly she moved!

CHAPTER | 6

Commas are like road signs. They give us direction, tell us where to pause, and make information clear to us. This chapter explains some of the ways to use commas in sentences.

MAKING SENSE OF SENTENCES WITH COMMAS

This chapter shows how to use commas to separate different parts of sentences. (As you go through this chapter, remember what you have already learned about sentences, sentence fragments, run-ons, and comma splices.) You will learn how to use commas to set off introductory sentence parts, explaining phrases, and nonessential clauses.

SETTING OFF INTRODUCTORY SENTENCE PARTS

Use a comma to set off introductory words, phrases, and clauses from the main part of a sentence. The comma keeps the reader from accidentally attaching the introductory portion to the main part of the sentence, then having to go back and reread the sentence. In other words, commas following introductory elements will save the reader time and reduce the chances of misinterpreting what is written. Read the examples below to see how introductory words, phrases, and clauses are set off with commas.

- **Words**

  Relieved, I gathered my things and left for the day.

  Surprised, I backed into a table.

  Amazed, the doctor revised his patient's medication.

- **Phrases**

  Hoping for the best, we checked our findings.

  Badly injured in the accident, Steve was hospitalized for three months.

  Fooled by the pitch, the batter missed the ball.

- **Clauses**

  When we looked more carefully, we located the missing order.

  Although the roads were icy, we arrived at work on time.

  Since we added staff, our workload has eased.

Introductory clauses are dependent clauses, because they cannot stand alone. In the clause examples above, the dependent clause is followed by a comma because it is introducing the rest of the sentence. If the two parts of each of these sentences were reversed, the sentence would still make sense. However, if you reverse the sentence parts, placing the dependent clause at the end, you do *not* need a comma.

We located the missing order when we looked more carefully.

We arrived at work on time although the roads were icy.

Our workload has eased since we added staff.

Practice

Use what you know about commas to correct these sentences. Check your work with the corrected versions at the end of the chapter.

1. Concerned about his future Brad went back to school.
2. Soaking in the stainless steel sink his shirt looked doomed.
3. I gathered all the supplies, before I started work this morning.
4. By repairing the equipment ourselves we saved several days.

5. Ecstatic the coach hugged the referee.

6. I will remember how to assemble this vacuum, as long as I have the directions.

7. As far as I know the guests in that room checked out an hour ago.

CLARIFYING MEANING

Commas help the reader to know which words belong together. Add commas to the following sentences to help make their meaning clear.

> Outside the yard was covered with flowers.
>
> After running the horses returned to the barn.
>
> During the night time drags on and on.
>
> As he watched the clock slowly ticked away the seconds.

The sentences should read like this:

> Outside, the yard was covered with flowers.
>
> After running, the horses returned to the barn.
>
> During the night, time drags on and on.
>
> As he watched, the clock slowly ticked away the seconds.

SETTING OFF EXPLAINING PHRASES

An **explaining phrase** is a word or group of words that immediately follows a noun or pronoun. The phrase makes the noun or pronoun clearer or more definite by explaining or identifying it. (An explaining phrase is also called an *appositive*.) Look at these examples. The explaining phrases have been highlighted.

> Mindy Wilcox ordered dinner, **a thick filet with steamed vegetables**.
>
> Melanie Hicklin, **our company nurse**, will give flu shots tomorrow.
>
> The keynote speaker is Mary Swenson, **director of the Animal Rescue League**.

Sometimes an identifying proper noun will precede or follow a common noun. If the proper noun is necessary to identify the person, place, or thing, it is not set off by commas. However, if the person can be identified without the proper noun, then the proper noun is surrounded by commas.

> My brother, **David,** farms and ranches in South Dakota.
>
> The shock rocker **Marilyn Manson** performed at the Civic Center.
>
> The vice-president, **Al Gore,** visited the flood site.

Any time information not essential to the meaning of a sentence is added, that information is set off by commas. Take the first sentence above, for example. The presence of commas tells us that the writer has only one brother. *David* is set off by commas because *brother* is enough information to identify the subject. The name David simply adds additional information. However, in the second example, we know that more than one shock rocker exists since the name Marilyn Manson is not set off by commas.

Practice

Use what you have learned to add commas to the following sentences. Check your work with the answers at the end of the chapter.

8. Air quality a major urban problem has steadily improved over the last few years.
9. Walter the featured artist delivered a stunning presentation.
10. Sharon spends Friday evenings at the movies an event she looks forward to all week.
11. Ms. Mason the route manager always leaves the papers at the corner.
12. My aunt Marsha will visit later this month. (The writer has only one aunt.)

ESSENTIAL CLAUSES

At the beginning of this chapter, you learned that an introductory dependent clause is followed by a comma, but that, when it is moved to the end of the sentence, no comma is needed. In some sentences a dependent clause cannot be omitted without changing the basic meaning of the sentence. Omitting it changes the meaning of the sentence or makes it untrue. Such a clause is an **essential clause** (also known as a restrictive clause) and is not set off by commas. You can see how this works in the following sentences.

All drivers **who have had a drunk driving conviction** should have their licenses revoked.

All drivers should have their licenses revoked.

The highlighted clause is essential because the meaning of the sentence is changed if the clause is removed from the sentence. The lack of commas shows that the clause is essential.

NONESSENTIAL CLAUSES

A **nonessential** clause adds information that is not essential to the basic meaning of the sentence. If a nonessential clause is removed, the basic meaning of the sentence is not changed. Nonessential clauses (also known as nonrestrictive clauses) are set off by commas. See how this works in the following examples.

> Matt's mother, **who has trouble with directions**, had to ask for help.
> Matt's mother had to ask for help.

The highlighted clause is nonessential because if it is removed from the sentence, the basic meaning of the sentence is not changed. To show that it is nonessential, it is set off by commas. Nonessential clauses usually begin with one of these words, which are called **subordinate conjunctions** (because they introduce dependent, or subordinate, clauses): *who, whom, whose, which,* or *that.*

Practice

Each of the following sentences contains a dependent clause, which is highlighted for you. If the clause is essential, do not add commas. If it is nonessential, set it off with commas. Check your work with the answers at the end of the chapter.

13. Mr. Lindgren is not a man **who likes to be fooled**.
14. Nicole lives on Briarwood Drive **which is south of the freeway**.
15. The cattle **that were vaccinated** are immune to mad cow disease.
16. Children **who are born on February 29** start school before they are two.
17. The mall restaurant offers free beverages to anyone **who orders a dinner**.
18. Josh **who is very outgoing** has become one of my best friends.

Review

It's time for a real challenge. This next exercise contains no commas, end marks, or capital letters. Use what you have learned so far to add capital letters, end marks, and commas to make sense of the paragraph. Check your work with the corrected version at the end of the chapter.

because mary and velma were morning people they met for breakfast every day before work they met at village inn on the corner of university ave and swanson blvd usually they had a light breakfast of bagels with cream cheese and coffee whenever one of them had something to celebrate they would order english muffins and omelettes something neither of them liked to make themselves how they enjoyed those mornings

they had a host of special rules regarding these special omelettes what were those rules if one of them was celebrating a birthday they ordered omelettes with something red such as tomatoes or red peppers mary's birthday was feb 22 velma's was oct 12 if one of them had received a raise they ordered omelettes with green peppers or green onions only once when velma won the lottery did they order omelettes with cheese and bacon

Answers

1. Concerned about his future, Brad went back to school.
2. Soaking in the stainless-steel sink, his shirt looked doomed.
3. I gathered all the supplies before I started work this morning.
4. By repairing the equipment ourselves, we saved several days.
5. Ecstatic, the coach hugged the referee.
6. I will remember how to assemble this vacuum as long as I have directions.
7. As far as I know, the guests in that room checked out an hour ago.
8. Air quality, a major urban problem, has steadily improved over the last few years.
9. Walter, the featured artist, delivered a stunning presentation.
10. Sharon spends Friday evenings at the movies, an event she looks forward to all week.
11. Ms. Mason, the route manager, always leaves the papers at the corner.
12. My aunt, Marsha, will visit later this month.
13. Essential clause. No commas needed.
14. Nicole lives on Briarwood Drive, which is south of the freeway.
15. Essential clause. No commas needed.

16. Essential clause. No commas needed.

17. Essential clause. No commas needed.

18. Josh, who is very outgoing, has become one of my best friends.

Review

Because Mary and Velma were morning people, they met for breakfast every day before work. They met at Village Inn on the corner of University Ave. and Swanson Blvd. Usually, they had a light breakfast of bagels with cream cheese and coffee. Whenever one of them had something to celebrate, they would order English muffins and omelettes, something neither of them liked to make themselves. How they enjoyed those mornings!

They had a host of special rules regarding these special omelettes. What were those rules? If one of them was celebrating a birthday, they ordered omelettes with something red, such as tomatoes or red peppers. Mary's birthday was Feb. 22; Velma's was Oct. 12. If one of them had received a raise, they ordered omelettes with green peppers or green onions. Only once, when Velma won the lottery, did they order omelettes with cheese and bacon.

CHAPTER | 7

Besides being road signs for sentences, commas also have many other jobs. This chapter explains other uses for commas and reviews what you learned about commas in Chapter 6.

MORE JOBS FOR COMMAS

As you know, commas are used to separate sentence parts in order to make the meaning of the sentence clear. In this chapter, you'll learn how to use commas to separate independent clauses, items in a series, items in a date or address, adjectives, contrasting elements, and words that interrupt the flow of thought in a sentence. You'll also learn how to use commas in a friendly letter.

SEPARATING INDEPENDENT CLAUSES

You already know that an independent clause is a group of words that could stand alone as a complete sentence. A conjunction is a joining word. Here is a complete list of conjunctions that can be used to join two independent clauses:

and	*for*	*so*
but	*nor*	*yet*
or		

When two or more independent clauses are joined with a conjunction to make a compound sentence, a comma should follow the first clause. The commas and conjunctions are highlighted in the following examples.

I wanted experience, **so** I fixed the printer myself.

Laura packed the glassware carefully, **but** some of it still broke during the move.

Mandy lost her purse, **and** her driver's license was in her wallet.

If independent clauses are joined **without** a conjunction, they are separated by a semicolon instead of a comma.

We told Mr. Kay about our plan; he wasn't sure it would work.

The company's finances have improved; we still need to spend carefully.

I found Susan's address; I hadn't seen her for months.

Practice

Use commas and semicolons to correctly punctuate the sentences below. Check your work with the answers at the end of the chapter.

1. Isaac started mowing the yard but his father finished it.
2. If you know of a good landscaper please give me the name of the company.
3. The furniture was covered with sheets yet it still became dusty and dirty.
4. Wayne likes Mike Oldfield he's an old New Age musician who's recorded a CD.
5. Edward knows what you want he just doesn't know where to find it.
6. Great things happen when we put our heads together.
7. The pilot was overcome with grief after the accident and he refused to fly again.
8. As you grow older your body absorbs fewer nutrients so many people take vitamin and mineral supplements.

SEPARATING ITEMS IN A SERIES

Separating a list of similar words, phrases, or clauses makes the material easier for the reader to understand. Usually, the last item in a series is preceded by a conjunction. No comma is needed before the conjunction. However, some writers prefer to use one because it helps to clarify some sentences.

> Cory, Sue, John, and Craig went to the conference.
>
> The horse snorted, pawed the dirt, reared up, and ran off toward hills.
>
> Sean taught me how to inventory the equipment, stock the shelves, and complete a quality-control check.

If each item in the series is separated by a conjunction, no commas are needed.

> Kara and Farrah and Andrea left their books behind.

SEPARATING ITEMS IN DATES AND ADDRESSES

When a year is specified in a date including the month and year, surround it with commas. If only the month or the season is listed, no commas are needed.

> Jody came to Fargo on June 1, 1997, right after she graduated from high school.
>
> Jody came to Fargo in June 1997 after graduating from high school.

When the name of a state is included to further identify a city, set it off with commas.

> Gail has lived in Peoria since last year.
>
> Gail has lived in Peoria, Illinois, since last year.

Practice

Add commas and end marks where they are needed in the following sentences. Remember what you learned in the last chapter about commas. Check your work with the answers at the end of the chapter.

9. Sally bought a kitchen table Hal bought an iron a toaster a blender and gas grill

10. Seeing no answer to the problem Jeff quit for the day and went home

11. Bernice was born November 3 1928 and Eugene was born January 17 1929

12. The gentleman living at 547 35th Street St. Louis Missouri collects oak barrels pickling crocks and colored glass jars

13. After running into a police car with his truck Adam used his cellular phone to call the police his doctor his lawyer and his insurance agent

SEPARATING EQUALLY IMPORTANT ADJECTIVES

An adjective is a word that modifies, or describes, a noun or pronoun. Adjectives answer the questions *Which one? What kind?* and *How many?* The highlighted words in the sentences below are adjectives.

Kathy avoided the **friendly, talkative, pleasant** boy sitting next to her at work. (The highlighted words describe *boy*. They answer the question *What kind?*)

The workmen repaired the floor with **that dark, aged oak** flooring. (The highlighted words describe *flooring*. They answer the questions *Which one?* and *What kind?*)

The reporter spoke with **several intense, talented high school** athletes. (The highlighted words describe athletes. They answer the questions *How many?* and *What kind?)*

When adjectives are equally important in describing a word, they are separated by a comma. However, not all adjectives are equally important. Some adjectives must be right next to the word they modify, or they will not make sense. For instance, in the second example sentence above, the word *oak* must be placed next to the word *flooring*.

Pay close attention to the last example sentence above. The words *several, high,* and *school* are all adjectives modifying *athletes,* but they are not separated by commas. These adjectives need to stay where they are in the sentence for the words to make sense, and they should not be separated by a comma from the word they modify. Only adjectives of equal importance are set off by a comma.

How can you tell if adjectives should be separated with a comma? Apply one or both of these tests:

1. Change the order of the adjectives. If the sentence reads just as clearly, separate the adjectives with a comma. If the sentence becomes unclear or sounds awkward, do not use a comma. The first two example sentences above make sense even if the position of the adjectives is changed.

   In the last example sentence above, the sentence would make no sense if the adjectives came in this order: *intense, three, high, talented, school. Intense* and *talented* are the only adjectives in the sentence that can be reversed; therefore, they are the only adjectives separated by a comma.

   Alex avoided the **pleasant, friendly, talkative** boy sitting next to him at work.

   The carpenter repaired the floor with that **aged, dark** oak flooring.

   The reporter spoke with several **talented, intense** high school athletes.

2. A second, equally effective test is to place the word *and* between the adjectives. If the sentence still reads well, use commas between the adjectives. If the sentence sounds unclear or awkward, do not use commas. Again, this works with the first two example sentences, but in the last sentence an *and* makes sense only between *intense* and *talented.*

   Alex avoided the **friendly and talkative and pleasant** boy sitting next to him at work.

   The carpenter repaired the floor with that **dark and aged** oak flooring.

   The reporter spoke with several **intense and talented** high school athletes.

Practice

Try these two tests with the following sentences. Where do the commas belong?

   Marshall cut his short wavy light blond hair.

   In my wallet are five crisp new twenty dollar bills.

The sentences should be punctuated like this:

> Marshall cut his **short, wavy** light blond hair.
>
> In my wallet are five **crisp, new** twenty dollar bills.

SEPARATING SENTENCE ELEMENTS

- Use commas to separate contrasting elements in a sentence. The following examples illustrate contrasting elements in a sentence. The comma tells the reader that what follows is an opposite idea. It makes the idea easier for the reader to grasp. The contrasting ideas are highlighted.

> We interviewed well, **but did poorly on the written test.**
>
> This company needs problem solvers, **not complainers**, to tackle our challenges.
>
> The liquid poured slowly at first, **quickly toward the end**.
>
> The tour group expected to meet the actors, **not a press agent**.

- Use commas to separate words or phrases that interrupt the flow of thought in a sentence. The words and phrases that interrupt the flow of thought in the sentences below have been highlighted.

> The task, **it seemed to us**, was overwhelming.
>
> The dog remembered, **however**, the harsh words and cruel actions of his owner.
>
> Morning, **we discovered**, was the best time to water the lawn.

- Whenever the name of the person being addressed is included in a sentence, it should be set off by commas. Jessi is the person being addressed in each of the following examples. Notice how commas are used to set off her name, depending on where it is placed in the sentence.

> **Jessi**, Pat needs you to sign for a package in the office before you leave.
>
> Pat needs you to sign for a package in the office, **Jessi**, before you leave.
>
> Pat needs you to sign for a package in the office before you leave, **Jessi**.

- Mild exclamations included in a sentence are also set off with commas. The exclamations have been highlighted for you in each of the following examples.

> **Gosh**, I never expected you'd make such a fuss.
>
> **No**, we won't be needing you any longer.
>
> **Heck**, we could have done that hours ago.

USING COMMAS IN A FRIENDLY LETTER

- Use a comma after the greeting of a friendly letter.

> Dear Aunt Hilda,
>
> Dear Juanita,
>
> Dear Val,

- Use a comma after the closing of a friendly letter.

> Sincerely yours,
>
> Yours truly,

Practice

Using what you have learned so far about commas and semicolons, correct these sentences. Check your work with the corrected versions of the sentences at the end of the chapter.

14. Exhausted from sitting rather than from physical exertion Ling sank into the soft green easy chair.
15. The Founders Day sale runs December 26 1997 through January 8 1998.
16. Suddenly the rope tore and the tire swing plummeted to the ground.
17. We're sorry Tom that you were inconvenienced and we'd like to make it up to you.
18. The new address if I'm remembering correctly is 1140 Westown Cole Illinois
19. When I travel I pack my toothbrush a hairbrush a shoe brush and a clothes brush.
20. Yes the sales department met their monthly goal over $200,000 in receipts they're celebrating right now!

Answers

1. Isaac started mowing the yard, but his father finished it.
2. If you know of a good landscaper, please give me the name of the company.
3. The furniture was covered with sheets, yet it still became dusty and dirty.
4. Wayne likes Mike Oldfield; he's an old New Age musician who's recorded a CD.
5. Edward knows what you want; he just doesn't know where to find it.
6. No change.
7. The pilot was overcome with grief after the accident, and he refused to fly again.
8. As you grow older, your body absorbs fewer nutrients, so many people take vitamin and mineral supplements.
9. Sally bought a kitchen table. Hal bought an iron, a toaster, a blender, and gas grill.
10. Seeing no answer to the problem, Jeff quit for the day and went home.
11. Bernice was born November 3, 1928, and Eugene was born January 17, 1929.
12. The gentleman living at 547 35th Street, St. Louis, Missouri, collects oak barrels, pickling crocks, and colored glass jars.
13. After running into a police car with his truck, Adam used his cellular phone to call the police, his doctor, his lawyer, and his insurance agent.
14. Exhausted from sitting, rather than from physical exertion, Ling sank into the soft, green easy chair.
15. The Founders Day sale runs December 26, 1997, through January 8, 1998.
16. Suddenly, the rope tore, and the tire swing plummeted to the ground.
17. We're sorry, Tom, that you were inconvenienced, and we'd like to make it up to you.
18. The new address, if I'm remembering correctly, is 1140 Westown, Cole, Illinois.

19. When I travel, I pack my toothbrush, a hairbrush, a shoe brush, and a clothes brush.

20. Yes, the sales department met their monthly goal, over $200,000 in receipts; they're celebrating right now!

CHAPTER | 8

Semicolons (;) and colons (:) confuse many writers. This chapter sorts it all out for you. By the time you finish, you'll know exactly how to use both.

GETTING FANCY WITH SEMICOLONS AND COLONS

In this chapter you will review what you have learned about punctuation so far, especially the use of semicolons to separate independent clauses. You will also learn how to use semicolons with certain joining words, and when to separate items in a series with semicolons. You will learn some of the uses of colons as well.

SEMICOLONS
SEPARATING INDEPENDENT CLAUSES

- Use a semicolon to separate independent clauses joined without a conjunction.

This rule may seem familiar to you because it was also included in Chapters 4 and 7. Refresh your memory by examining these example sentences.

Three people built the model; only one received credit for it.

Work at straightening out these shelves; someone else will get the floors.

Your time is up; you need to move on to the next project.

- Use a semicolon to separate independent clauses that contain commas, even if the clauses are joined by a conjunction.

The accounting department needed better equipment, updated training, and sound professional advice; but since all of this came after the audit, the books were in sorry shape.

In this complex-compound sentence, the semicolon helps the reader see where the break in thought occurs. The semicolon makes the sentence easier to understand.

- Use a semicolon to separate independent clauses connected with a conjunctive adverb that expresses a relationship between clauses (see Chapter 4). When words such as *however, therefore, then,* and *thus* connect two independent clauses, the first independent clause is followed by a semicolon, and the joining word is followed by a comma. Look at the following examples to see how this is done.

We ordered from last year's catalog; **consequently,** our prices were wrong.

I wanted a new sports car; **however,** my bank account wouldn't support one.

My sister Dorothy thought she was cheated; **therefore,** she wanted her money back.

In the movie *Star Wars,* Luke Skywalker searches for a mysterious princess; **furthermore,** he destroys an evil Death Star.

Here is a list of these special joining words:

accordingly	however	then
besides	instead	therefore
consequently	moreover	thus
furthermore	nevertheless	
hence	otherwise	

It's easy to confuse these conjunctive adverbs with subordinate conjunctions such as *because, although, since, until,* and *while.* Subordinate conjunctions introduce dependent clauses that cannot stand alone as a sentence. The conjunctive adverbs, however, introduce independent clauses that can stand alone without the adverb.

Here's an easy test to see if the word beginning a clause is a subordinate conjunction, for which you need only a comma, or a conjunctive adverb that needs a semicolon: If you can move the word around in the clause, it's the joining word that takes a semicolon. If not, it's probably a subordinate conjunction. Let's try the test with the two independent clauses below.

My paycheck was late. I couldn't pay my rent on time.

Here are two different ways of combining these two independent clauses.

My paycheck was late; therefore, I couldn't pay my rent on time.

I couldn't pay my rent on time because my paycheck was late.

In the first sentence, you could move *therefore* to a different place in the clause if you wanted to. You could say, "I couldn't, therefore, pay my rent on time." So, *therefore* is a conjunctive adverb.

In the second sentence, the word *because* makes no sense anywhere else in the clause. You wouldn't say, "My paycheck because was late." Therefore, *because* is a subordinate conjunction.

SEPARATING ITEMS IN A SERIES

Use a semicolon to separate items in a series if the items contain commas. This helps the reader to see which sets of items go together. Unlike items in a series separated by commas, a semicolon is used even when there *is* a conjunction.

The possible dates for the potluck are Thursday, June 5; Saturday, June 7; Sunday, June 8; or Monday, June 9.

On our team you'll find the hustlers, Jake and Marilynn; the slackers, Henrietta, Chuck, and Kerald; and the easy-going people, Judy, Rob, and Kirsten.

The packing plant will relocate in either Fort Madison, Iowa; Omaha, Nebraska; or Sioux Falls, South Dakota.

Practice

Use what you have learned to add commas and semicolons to the following sentences. Check your work with the answers at the end of the chapter.

1. Helen left her desk unlocked at work consequently she worried about it all night.
2. The menu included broiled salmon steamed broccoli grilled potatoes spinach and bread but for some reason they served no dessert.
3. Tim hurried through his work however he still wasn't finished by 8:30.
4. The bus traveled through Chicago Illinois Dayton Ohio and Pittsburgh Pennsylvania.
5. I've been at this for two days I need to get away for a while.

COLONS
COLONS THAT INTRODUCE

- Use a colon to introduce a list of items.

    These people were transferred: Audrey, Brett, Bradley, and Lindsay.

    We ordered these supplies: paper, staplers, scissors, markers, and tape.

Do not use a colon if the list of items completes the meaning begun by the verb, in other words, if it fits right into the flow of the sentence. Here are the above example sentences, rewritten in such a way that a colon is not necessary.

    The people transferred were Audrey, Brett, Bradley, and Lindsay.

    We ordered paper, staplers, scissors, markers, and tape.

- Use a colon to introduce a formal quotation.

  Nietzsche offered this sound advice: "Smash not the happy delusions of men."

- Use a colon to introduce a word, phrase, or clause that adds particular emphasis to the main body of a sentence.

  Your busy work schedule is the result of one thing: poor planning.

  Jerry needed this essential information: the price.

COLONS THAT SHOW RELATIONSHIP

Use a colon to show a relationship in the following cases:

- Between two independent clauses when the second explains the first.

  Judy shouted and turned cartwheels: She had just finished the last page of the report.

  Brian framed the paycheck: It was the first check he had ever earned.

  Sylvia ignored the doorbell: She knew it was a salesman she had no time for.

- Between the title and the subtitle of a book.

  Measurement: Translating into Metric

  Next Step: A Futuristic View of Technology

  Fear: Tales from the Dark Side

- Between volumes and page numbers.

  Contemporary Authors V:128

  Education Digest 10:23

  Marvel Comics 21:24

- Between chapters and verses.

  James 3:10

  Exodus 1:1

  Proverbs 2:2

- Between hours and minutes.

  12:53 a.m.

  2:10 p.m.

USING COLONS IN BUSINESS LETTERS

You learned in Chapter 7 that a comma follows the greeting (or salutation) in a personal, or friendly, letter. In business communications, a colon signals the reader that what follows is a business matter, something to be taken seriously. This is particularly true if you include the position, but not the name of the person to whom the letter is addressed. However, even in a business letter the closing is followed by a comma.

Dear Ms. Essian:
Sincerely yours,

Dear Editor:
Cordially yours,

Practice

Practice what you have learned about commas, semicolons, and colons by adding them to the following sentences. Check your work with the answers at the end of the chapter.

6. Hammond located the procedure in the policy manual Volume 6 89.
7. The hail destroyed all of the wheat however the corn was untouched by the violent storm.
8. Before I bought a new car I did some research in the library checked out the local car dealerships asked a few friends for advice and consulted my mechanic.
9. Dear Customer
    Your order should arrive on or before January 5 1997.
    Sincerely yours
10. Each day a new shift begins at 8 30 a.m. 4 30 p.m. and 12 30 a.m.
11. Megan likes to play soccer a physically challenging sport bridge a game of logic and strategy Street Fighter a mindless Super Nintendo game and the harmonica an invigorating instrument.
12. The police learned the following information from the interrogation the suspect's name the suspect's home address the suspect's phone number and his current employer.

Answers

1. Helen left her desk unlocked at work; consequently, she worried about it all night.

2. The menu included broiled salmon, steamed broccoli, grilled potatoes, spinach, and bread; but for some reason they served no dessert.

3. Tim hurried through his work; however, he still wasn't finished by 8:00.

4. The bus traveled through Chicago, Illinois; Dayton, Ohio; and Pittsburgh, Pennsylvania.

5. I've been at this for two days; I need to get away for a while.

6. Hammond located the procedure in the policy manual Volume 6: 89.

7. The hail destroyed all of the wheat; however, the corn was untouched by the violent storm.

8. Before I bought a new car, I did some research in the library, checked out the local car dealerships, asked a few friends for advice, and consulted my mechanic.

9. Dear Customer:
   Your order should arrive on or before January 5, 1997.
   Sincerely yours,

10. Each day a new shift begins at 8:30 a.m., 4:30 p.m., and 12:30 a.m.

11. Megan likes to play soccer, a physically challenging sport; bridge, a game of logic and strategy; Street Fighter, a mindless Super Nintendo game; and the harmonica, an invigorating instrument.

12. The police learned the following information from the interrogation: the suspect's name, the suspect's home address, the suspect's phone number, and his current employer.

CHAPTER | 9

This chapter explains the knotty problems of quotation marks, both double and single. By the time you finish, you'll be in control of quotation marks in your writing.

CONTROLLING QUOTATION MARKS

Quotation marks pose a problem for many writers, but a few simple rules can make them easy to use. Although these marks are most often found in dialogue, other writing situations require them as well.

USING QUOTATION MARKS IN DIRECT QUOTATIONS

- Use double quotation marks to set off a direct quotation or thought within a sentence or paragraph. This includes quotations that are signed, etched, inscribed, carved, etc.

The managers called our new pricing policy "the innovation of the decade."

We thought he said, "Turn right at the corner."

The sign read, "No Smoking."

"Eccentric and Erratic," the headstone read.

- Do not use quotation marks for a paraphrase, or the restatement of a direct quotation or thought in other words. The examples below illustrate the difference.

    We thought he said, "Turn right at the corner." (direct quotation)

    We thought he said to turn right at the corner. (paraphrase)

    "When will help arrive?" I wondered. (direct thought)

    I wondered when help would arrive. (paraphrase of a thought)

    The sign clearly read, "No Smoking." (signed words)

    The sign said not to smoke. (paraphrase)

- Use single quotation marks to set off a quotation within a quotation.

    "Jane heard her say, 'The delivery is scheduled for 9:00.'" said Florence.

    The lecturer continued, "Remember the salesman's motto: 'You can't sell it if your pitch is lousy.'"

    Our doctor always says, "Haven't I told you my mother's famous words: 'Healthy mind, healthy body'?"

USING QUOTATION MARKS IN DIALOGUE

Correctly punctuating dialogue means understanding how to use quotation marks, commas, and end marks. Take a close look at the sentences in the dialogue sample below: They include the basic dialogue structures. The words quoted are called *quotations,* and the words explaining who said the quotations are called *tags.* In the examples below, the tags are highlighted.

"I'm really hungry. I want something to eat," **said Harry.**

Nina answered, "I'm hungry, but I don't have any cash. Do you have some?"

"What is this?" **Harry asked.** "You're the one with the manager's job."

"Yes," **Nina said,** "but credit cards are all I ever carry."

Quoted words are always surrounded by quotation marks. Place quotation marks before a group of quoted words and again at the end. Tags are punctuated differently depending on where they are in the sentence.

- If the tag follows a quotation, and the quotation is a sentence normally ending with a period, use a comma instead. The period comes at the end of the tag. (See the first example sentence, above.)

  However, if the quotation is a sentence normally ending with a question mark or an exclamation point, insert the question mark or exclamation point. Place a period after the tag, but do not use a comma. The examples below illustrate these rules.

  "I'm really hungry. Let's grab something to eat," said David.

  "I'm really hungry. Do you want to grab something to eat?" asked David.

  "I'm really hungry. Hold it—a Bonanza!" exclaimed David.

- When the tag comes before the quotation, place a comma after the tag. Put quotation marks around the quoted words, capitalize the first word of the quotation, and punctuate the sentence as you would normally, as in the sentences below.

  David said, "I'm really hungry. Let's grab something to eat."

  David said, "I'm really hungry. Do you want to grab something to eat?"

  David said, "I'm really hungry. Hold it—a Bonanza!"

- Sometimes, the tag interrupts the quotation. If both the first and second parts of the quotation are complete sentences, the first part of the quotation is punctuated in the same way as a quotation with the tag at the end. In other words, the period follows the tag. The rest of the quotation is punctuated in the same way as a quotation preceded by a tag. See the example sentences below.

  "I'm really hungry," said David. "Let's grab something to eat."

  "Do you want to grab something to eat?" David asked. "I'm really hungry."

  "Hold it—a Bonanza!" exclaimed David. "I'm really hungry."

- When the tag interrupts a sentence, the words preceding the tag begin the thought, and the words following the tag complete the thought. Place quotation marks around the quoted words and follow the first part of the quotation with a comma. Place a comma after the tag—not a period, since the sentence is not completed. Place quotation marks around the last part of the quotation, but *do not* capitalize the first letter of the quotation, as it is not the beginning of a new sentence. Punctuate the rest of the sentence as you would normally. See the example sentences below.

  "The Carters just don't understand," observed Solomon, "why they upset you so."

  "This lawn care service," explained Alvin, "provides fertilizer, seed, and weed control."

  "What I can't see," mused Mel, "is what you see in him."

Note: All of the punctuation is *inside* the quotation marks except for the punctuation marks following the tags.

DIALOGUE AT A GLANCE

- Tags following a quotation:

  "_____," said Rose.

  "_____?" asked Rose.

  "_____!" exclaimed Rose.

- Tags preceding a quotation:

  Iris said, "_____."

  Iris asked, "_____?"

  Iris exclaimed, "_____!"

- Tags between two sentences of a quotation:

  "_____," said Lily. "_____."

  "_____?" asked Lily. "_____?"

  "_____!" exclaimed Lily. "_____!"

- Tags interrupting a one-sentence quotation:

  "_____," said Daisy, "_____."

  "_____," asked Daisy, "_____?"

  "_____," exclaimed Daisy, "_____!"

OTHER USES FOR QUOTATION MARKS

- Use quotation marks to set off nicknames and words used as slang.

  Kristy was dubbed "Miss Hustle" by her teammates.

  All the kids said the new CD was really "bad."

- Use quotation marks to indicate irony or raised eyebrows. Avoid overusing quotation marks in this way. It doesn't work if you do it all the time.

  My yearly "evaluation" involved a three-minute conversation with the boss.

  That "consultant" offered no advice or counsel.

  Their idea of a "good time" is popcorn and a movie.

- Use quotation marks to set off titles of certain items. Other titles should be italicized. See the table on this page for the differences.

Enclose in Quotation Marks	Italicize
name of a short story or chapter of a book	title of a novel
name of a TV program	name of a movie
title of a poem	title of a collection of poetry or an epic poem
headline of an article or title of a report	name of a magazine or newspaper
title of a song	title of a musical or long musical composition
	name of a ship, plane, train, etc.

ITALICS INSTEAD OF QUOTATION MARKS

Italics are used instead of quotation marks for titles of the items in the second column of the above table. They are also used when referring to words as words, and for emphasis:

Words as words:

The word *food* always brought a smile to his face.

Emphasis:

I have *never* seen anyone so fond of music.

QUOTATION MARKS WITH OTHER PUNCTUATION MARKS

Here are the rules for combining quotation marks with other punctuation marks:

- Question marks, exclamation points, and dashes go *inside* quotation marks if they are part of a quotation. If they are not, place them *outside* the quotation marks.

    The dentist asked, "Can you feel me probing in this area?" (part of the quotation)

    Did you watch last week's "Seinfeld"? (not part of the quotation)

    "I wish I'd never heard of—" Calvin stopped suddenly as Kelly entered the room. (part of the quotation)

    My favorite song will always be "The Rose"! (not part of the quotation)

- Periods and commas go *inside* closing quotation marks.

    "Wait for half an hour," suggested Dalia, "before you go swimming."

- Colons and semicolons go *outside* closing quotation marks.

    Here's how I felt about last week's "Friends": I loved it.

    The interviewer dismissed the remark as a "slip of the tongue"; the guest was insulted.

Practice

Use what you have learned about quotation marks to correct the following sentences. Check your work with the answers at the end of the chapter.

1. Do you ever watch Touched by an Angel on CBS? asked Steven.
2. Which one of you called me a cowardly excuse for a soldier? barked the sergeant.
3. After reading To Kill a Mockingbird, I rented the movie.
4. An extra five minutes at lunch was our prize.
5. All the teenagers at the party were duded out.
6. If you want to know why I'm so bitter, read my article Rosy Glasses in the latest copy of our newsletter, The Tower.
7. I wish that old fussbudget—Melanie stopped abruptly as Mr. Harris walked into the room.
8. Do you call everyone by the name Bubba asked Katie.
9. The investigator asked us where we had spent the evening.
10. Don't make outrageous excuses my attorney advised that will only make matters worse.
11. Ebenezer said I told you the representative said No way before I ever had a chance to explain.
12. Why are you still here my supervisor asked everyone else went home an hour ago.
13. We were shocked by our Christmas bonus a bag with a cookie and an orange.
14. Looking at her tardy record, I see why you've named her Punctual Paula.
15. Get out of the way yelled the captain.

Answers

1. "Do you ever watch 'Touched by an Angel' on CBS?" asked Steven.
2. "Which one of you called me a 'cowardly excuse for a soldier'?" barked the sergeant.
3. After reading *To Kill a Mockingbird*, I rented the movie.
4. An extra five minutes at lunch was our "prize."
5. All the teenagers at the party were "duded out."
6. If you want to know why I'm so bitter, read my article "Rosy Glasses" in the latest copy of our newsletter, *The Tower*.
7. "I wish that old fussbudget—" Melanie stopped abruptly as Mr. Harris walked into the room.
8. "Do you call everyone by the name 'Bubba'?" asked Katie.
9. No change.
10. "Don't make outrageous excuses," my attorney advised. "That will only make matters worse."
11. Ebenezer said, "I told you the representative said, 'No way!' before I ever had a chance to explain."
12. "Why are you still here?" my supervisor asked. "Everyone else went home an hour ago."
13. We were shocked by our Christmas "bonus": a bag with a cookie and an orange.
14. Looking at her tardy record, I see why you've named her "Punctual Paula."
15. "Get out of the way!" yelled the captain.

CHAPTER | 10

This chapter puts you in command of apostrophes and dashes, the most commonly misused marks of punctuation.

THE MYSTERIES OF APOSTROPHES AND DASHES

Apostrophes communicate important information in written language. Dashes, when used sparingly, add emphasis. The first part of this chapter covers the rules regarding apostrophes. The last part covers dashes.

APOSTROPHES
USING APOSTROPHES TO SHOW POSSESSION

Apostrophes are used to show that one or more things belong to one or more people or things. Apostrophes are often used because they shorten sentences, meaning fewer words for the reader. The following sets of examples illustrate this.

These toys belong to the boy.
These are the **boy's** toys.

We must find the weaknesses of the structure.
We must find the **structure's** weaknesses.

Listen to the complaints of these customers.
Listen to the **customers'** complaints.

Changing the location of an apostrophe can change the meaning of a sentence. Look at each of the sentences below. The words in parentheses explain what the apostrophe means.

These are the **boy's** toys. (The toys belong to one boy.)
These are the **boys'** toys. (The toys belong to more than one boy.)

We must find the **structure's** weaknesses. (One structure has weaknesses.)
We must find the **structures'** weaknesses. (Several structures have weaknesses.)

Listen to the **customer's** complaints. (One customer has several complaints.)
Listen to the **customers'** complaints. (Several customers have complaints.)

The position of the apostrophe tells the reader whether one person or thing possesses something, or if it's more than one person or thing doing the possessing. That is, it tells whether the word that possesses is singular (referring to one) or plural (referring to more than one).

- Add **'s** to singular words not ending in *s*.
    child's play
    king's palace
    lady's coat
    dentist's aide

- Add **'s** to singular words ending in *s*.
    Garth **Brooks's** latest recording
    American **Express's** advertising campaign
    Lois's birth certificate

- Add **s'** to plural words ending in *s*.
    girls' bicycles
    kids' books
    ladies' garments
    employees' agreement

- Add **'s** to plural words not ending in *s*.
    women's plans
    children's bedrooms
    men's shoes
    people's election

When a common or proper noun is more than one word, special rules apply. Usually, you add the *'s* to the last word in the noun

- Add **'s** to the last word of a compound noun.
    mother-in-law's visit
    president-elect's decision
    manager-in-training's duties

- Add **'s** to the last word of the name of a business or institution.
    Proctor and **Gamble's** products
    First State **Bank's** new hours
    Banton and Barton **Co.'s** president

- Add **'s** to the last name if a single item belongs to more than one person.
    Wayne and **Judy's** log home
    the receptionist and **secretary's** printer
    Mr. and Mrs. **Mitchell's** car

- Add an apostrophe to words showing periods of time if they show possession.

  > one **day's** schedule
  > one **year's** salary
  > three **days'** wait

- Add an apostrophe to words showing amounts of money if they show possession.

  > two **cents'** worth
  > a **dollar's** serial number
  > a **penny's** value

USING APOSTROPHES TO SHOW OMISSION

Use an apostrophe to show that letters or numbers have been omitted.

> Becky **doesn't** (does not) work today.
> The doctor **couldn't** (could not) give me a prescription.
> **Who's** (who is) on first?
> I **can't** (cannot) get together tomorrow afternoon.
> My first car was a **'67** (1967) Chevy.
> Uncle Louis tells lies about life in the **'50s** (1950s).

WHEN NOT TO USE APOSTROPHES

- Do not use an apostrophe to form a plural, but only to show possession for either singular or plural words.

  > **Wrong:** Get the tomatoe's from the garden.
  > **Correct:** Trim the **tomatoes'** lower limbs.

  > **Wrong:** Read the nutrition label on this bag of chip's.
  > **Correct:** Read the bag of **chips'** nutrition label.

- Do not use an apostrophe with words that already show possession (*my, mine, our, ours, your, yours, his, her, hers, their, theirs*). Note that these words do not have apostrophes in the examples below.

  > This is their boat. The boat is **theirs**. (no apostrophe)
  > We brought our grill. The grill is **ours**. (no apostrophe)
  > This experiment must be **yours**. (no apostrophe)

Practice

Practice what you have learned about apostrophes and other punctuation marks to correct the following sentences. Check your work with the answers at the end of the chapter.

1. Mr. Jones grocery has better produce than Mrs. Smiths.
2. Comp USAs top-selling product is Microns latest MMX computer.
3. Janices and Jays horse was named the Grand Champion Stud.
4. After six weeks steady work we earn a permanent position and a days paid vacation.
5. The picnic basket is their's.
6. Our firms territory has doubled in the last six months and the responsibility is your's.
7. Every Saturday noon the Womens Issues Group meets for lunch.
8. Bonnie works as a dentists assistant.
9. Employees motivations differ from an owners.
10. A managers reward is different from an employees.

DASHES

A dash is a specialized punctuation mark reserved for only a few situations. However, many writers use it incorrectly in place of other marks. Dashes call attention to themselves. Because of this, a careful writer uses them sparingly. They are very effective if used correctly, but they lose their impact if they are overused.

- Use a dash to mark a sudden break in thought or to insert a comment.

    Take these files and this—Look out for that truck!

    I remember the day—what teenager doesn't—that the space shuttle exploded.

    Abby is delighted—as we are—about your new job.

- Use a dash to emphasize explanatory material. You don't have to use a dash, but you may.

    Realizing your limitations—time, money, and energy—makes planning more realistic.

    He lit a cigarette inside the building—an unconscious habit.

- Use a dash to indicate omitted letters.

  "Oh, sh—, I lost the code for the copier!"

  He had received a letter from Mrs. N—.

- Use a dash to connect a beginning phrase to the rest of the sentence.

  Diversity and challenge—these are the advantages of our new programming.

  Albany, New York, and Trenton, New Jersey—that's where our current staff will be relocating.

Practice

Use what you know about dashes to correctly punctuate the following sentences. Check your work with the answers at the end of the chapter.

11. To run or to hide those were her only choices.
12. Our idea just in case you're interested is to remove the plastic coating.
13. Mr. O'Dea is the most unreasonable I should keep my opinions to myself.
14. Ted can never find his d pocket organizer when he Oh, now he's got it.
15. Intelligence, perseverance, and luck that's what you'll need for this job.

Review

Practice what you have learned about punctuation so far by adding capitalization, end marks, commas, semicolons, colons, apostrophes, and dashes to the following sentences. Check your work on these complicated sentences with the corrected versions at the end of the chapter.

16. though it is hard to understand my partners purpose in interviewing dr e s sanders jr was to eliminate him as a suspect in the crime
17. before hitting the ambulance at the corner of woodland and vine ms anderson saw a dark hooded figure crawl through the window reach back grab a small parcel and run north on vine
18. As the detective interrogated each of the boys and their fathers they determined that the mens stories did not match up with the boys versions

19. please bring these items when you drive up here tomorrow barbaras sleeping bag another can of avon insect repellent the girls queen-sized air mattress they want to use it to sunbathe on the water and my swimming trunks

20. karl malone and john stockton these two make an exciting combination a mixture of malones aggressiveness and stocktons finesse

Answers

1. Mr. Jones's grocery has better produce than Mrs. Smith's.
2. Comp USA's top-selling product is Micron's latest MMX computer.
3. Janice and Jay's horse was named the Grand Champion Stud.
4. After six weeks' steady work, we earn a permanent position and a day's paid vacation.
5. The picnic basket is theirs.
6. Our firm's territory has doubled in the last six months, and the responsibility is yours.
7. Every Saturday noon, the Women's Issues Group meets for lunch.
8. Bonnie works as a dentist's assistant.
9. Employees' motivations differ from an owner's.
10. A manager's reward is different from an employee's.
11. To run or to hide—those were her only choices.
12. Our idea—just in case you're interested—is to remove the plastic coating.
13. Mr. O'Dea is the most unreasonable—I should keep my opinions to myself.
14. Ted can never find his d— pocket organizer when he— Oh, now he's got it.
15. Intelligence, perseverance, and luck—that's what you'll need for this job.
16. Though it is hard to understand, my partner's purpose in interviewing Dr. E. S. Sanders, Jr., was to eliminate him as a suspect in the crime.
17. Before hitting the ambulance at the corner of Woodland and Vine, Ms. Anderson saw a dark, hooded figure crawl through the window, reach back, grab a small parcel, and run north on Vine.

18. As the detectives interrogated each of the boys and their fathers, they determined that the men's stories did not match up with the boys' versions.

19. Please bring these items when you drive up here tomorrow: Barbara's sleeping bag, another can of Avon insect repellent, the girls' queen-sized air mattress—they want to use it to sunbathe on the water—and my swimming trunks.

20. Karl Malone and John Stockton—these two make an exciting combination, a mixture of Malone's aggressiveness and Stockton's finesse.

CHAPTER 11

THE FINER POINTS OF PUNCTUATION

Most people misuse hyphens once in a while. Maybe you're one who does it often! Parentheses and diagonal slashes also cause problems, littering your written work like blemishes on an otherwise handsome face. This chapter explains when to use the less-often-used (and more often misused) punctuation marks and, as a bonus, explains how to write numbers.

The punctuation marks covered in this lesson—hyphens, parentheses, and diagonal marks—serve very specific purposes. Knowing and understanding their functions gives a writer an advantage in communicating ideas. This chapter explains how to use these marks. The last part of the chapter discusses using numbers in writing.

HYPHENS

The main purpose of a hyphen is to join words to create a compound word, which is a combination of words used as one word. Compound words may be written in three ways: as a single word, as two words, or as a hyphenated word. Whenever you are in doubt, consult a recent dictionary.

Since language changes constantly, a word written as two words often evolves into a hyphenated word, then eventually becomes a single word. For example, the word *semicolon* began as two separate words (*semi colon*). In the late fifties, dictionaries began listing it as a hyphenated word (*semi-colon*). A recent dictionary will list it as a single word (*semicolon*).

Two-Word Compound Nouns
couch potato

hat rack

window box

guitar pick

eye glasses

Hyphenated Compound Nouns
mother-in-law

vice-president-elect

secretary-treasurer

merry-go-round

problem-solver

player-manager

Single-Word Compound Nouns
doorbell

snowman

walkway

pantyhose

storeroom

batboy

- Use a hyphen to join two words working together as one.
    Mark is a **singer-dancer.**
    Pete Rose was a **player-coach** for the Cincinnati Reds.
    Mel Gibson has joined the ranks of well-known **actor-directors.**

- Use a hyphen to join more than two words into a single word.
    know-it-all
    good-for-nothing
    five-year-old

- Use a hyphen to join two or more words that function as a single modifying word. If the modifying words follow the word they modify, the modifying words are not hyphenated. Pay special attention to how these hyphenated adjectives are used when they follow the nouns they modify.
    An **ill-trained** evaluator causes more problems than no evaluator at all.
    The evaluator was **ill trained**.

    Management and the union finally agreed after months of **hard-nosed** negotiations.
    The negotiations were **hard nosed**.

Note: Some hyphenated adjectives, such as *old-fashioned* and *ladder-back*, and the words in the following section, keep their hyphens no matter where they are in a sentence. Check a recent dictionary when in doubt.

- Use a hyphen to join prefixes such as *self, half, ex, all, great, post, pro, former,* and *vice* or the suffix *elect* to words.
    The President unveiled the **all-powerful** orbiting space station.
    Lee Iacocca is a **self-made** man.
    You need to keep your **half-baked** plans a secret.
    Bobby saw his **ex-wife** leaving the drug store.
    Max's **great-grandfather** passed away on Wednesday.
    Senior citizens remember the **post-war** years with great fondness.
    The plans were ratified as soon as the **vice-president** saw them.
    The **treasurer-elect** picked up all the records from the presiding treasurer.

- Use a hyphen to avoid confusing or awkward spellings.

    The committee's job was to re-pair [not *repair*]the tournament participants.

    My mother decided to re-cover [not *recover*] her old rocking chair.

    The doorway had a bell-like [not *belllike*] shape.

    The accountant re-examined [not *reexamined*] the final totals.

- Use a hyphen to join a capital letter to a word.

    After that you'll see a T-intersection.

    Turn right at the first road after the S-curve.

    The carpenter used a T-square.

- Use a hyphen to write two-word numbers between 21 and 99 as words.

    forty-five

    sixty-four

    twenty-six

- Use a hyphen to join fractions written as words.

    three-fifths

    five-eighths

- Use a hyphen to join numbers to words used as a single adjective.

    three-year term

    eight-foot wall

    two-pronged fork

    forty-two-year-old man

Note: When a series of similar number-word adjectives is written in a sentence, use a hyphen/comma combination with all but the last item in the series.

    Plywood comes in **two-, four-,** and **six-foot** sheets.

    Joe scored three touchdowns on **twelve-, sixteen-,** and **five-yard** carries.

- Use a hyphen to join numbers indicating a life span, a score, or the duration of an event.

   > William Shakespeare (1564-1616) is the most widely read English writer.

   > The Cyclones won the game 78-67.

   > The speech should last 5-7 minutes.

- Use a hyphen to separate a word between syllables at the end of a line. Here are a few guidelines for dividing words:

   > Never leave a single-letter syllable on a line.

   > Divide hyphenated words at the hyphen.

   > Never divide a one-syllable word.

   > Avoid dividing words that have fewer than six letters.

   > Avoid dividing the last word of a paragraph.

   > Avoid dividing a number.

   > *When in doubt, always check a dictionary.*

Practice

Add hyphens where they are needed in the following sentences. Check your work with the answers at the end of the chapter.

1. After examining your brain X rays, I see little justification for you to act like a know it all.
2. Sister Linda May, now an ex nun, re evaluated her theology and became a pro life activist.
3. Eileen's well researched presentation impressed the audience of twenty five.
4. Allison's time in the one hundred meter dash beat mine by three tenths of a second.
5. After a day long business venture involving a water stand, the seven year old twins had made a ten cent profit.

PARENTHESES

- Use parentheses to enclose explanatory material that interrupts the normal flow of the sentence and is only marginally related to the text. Note: Parentheses are often interchangeable with dashes in this kind of sentence (see Chapter 10).

Center Street (a party neighborhood if there ever was one) is a great place to live.

The neighbors had a picnic on Fourth of July. (Fortunately, we were invited.)

Unfortunately, another set of neighbors (they were not invited) called the police to complain about the noise (probably that of the illegal fireworks).

We party-goers (how were we to know?) were completely surprised by the officers.

Notice the last three sentences. Each set of parentheses contains a complete sentence. If the parenthetical construction comes at the end of a sentence, it is punctuated as its own sentence within the parentheses. On the other hand, if it comes within another sentence, no capital letters or periods are necessary. However, if the parenthetical construction in the middle of another sentence is a sentence that would normally require a question mark or exclamation point, include that punctuation.

- Use parentheses to enclose information when accuracy is essential.

  The twin children of the deceased couple (Alma and Otto Priggi) requested an autopsy.

  The client agrees to pay the sum of two hundred twenty-five dollars ($225) per hour.

DIAGONAL MARK

Much like the hyphen, a diagonal mark (also called a solidus or a slant mark) is used to join words or numbers. The most frequent use of the diagonal is with the words *and/or,* which shows that the sentence refers to one or both of the words being joined.

  The cast will consent to interviews on radio and/or TV.

  Applesauce and/or blended fruits can replace oil in most cake recipes.

- Use a diagonal mark to separate numbers in a fraction.

  It takes us 4 1/2 hours to do the inventory at the end of the week.

  He'll want a 1 5/8-inch wrench for this nut.

NUMBERS

In newspaper writing, figures, or numerals, are used instead words because they are easier to identify and read. However, a number at the beginning of a sentence is always written as a word. In more formal writing, follow these rules.

- If a number can be written as one or two words, write it as a word. Otherwise, write the numeral.

  We saw fifteen safety movies last year.

  We saw 115 safety movies last year.

  The student wrote "I will not talk in class" three hundred times.

  The student wrote "I will not talk in class" 350 times.

- Use Arabic numerals (1, 2, 25) rather than Roman numerals (I, II, XXV) .

- Always write a number at the beginning of sentence as a word even if it is more than two words.

  One hundred twenty-five employees received year-end bonuses.

Practice

Use what you have learned about punctuation and capitalization to correct the following sentences. Check your work with the answers at the end of the chapter.

6. our new four wheel drive vehicle I have never liked Jeeps is in the shop again
7. sugar ray leonard what kind of name is sugar fought his way out of retirement several times
8. on delivery the recipient will pay the agreed on fee $435.67
9. employees bonuses will be time and or money for 2 5 of our staff
10. 4 of the workers who received pink slips will be re evaluated

Answers

1. After examining your brain X-rays, I see little justification for you to act like a know-it-all.

2. Sister Linda May, now an ex-nun, re-evaluated her theology and became a pro-life activist.

3. Eileen's well-researched presentation impressed the audience of twenty-five.

4. Allison's time in the one-hundred-meter dash beat mine by three-tenths of a second.

5. After a day-long business venture involving a water stand, the seven-year-old twins had made a ten-cent profit.

6. Our new four-wheel-drive vehicle (I have never liked Jeeps) is in the shop again.

7. Sugar Ray Leonard (what kind of name is "Sugar"?) fought his way out of retirement several times.

8. On delivery, the recipient will pay the agreed-on fee ($435.67).

9. Employees' bonuses will be time and/or money for two-fifths of our staff.

10. Four of the workers who received pink slips will be re-evaluated.

CHAPTER | 12

Verbs—words that show
action or a state of
being—drive written
language and give it life.
Because verbs are so
important, mistakes
involving verbs can be
glaring. This chapter
explains how to use verbs
correctly in sentences.

VERBS THAT FOLLOW THE RULES

Writers use words to communicate.
Few things are more confusing to the reader than misusing words—especially verbs. Incorrect verb forms call special attention to themselves. This lesson explains how to use regular verbs correctly and highlights of few of the most common mistakes writers make.

Read the paragraph on the next page. This letter contains several errors in verb tense. Can you spot them? By the end of this chapter, you'll probably be able to correct them all.

Ben had an accident today. He and I were haul a load of furniture from the warehouse. As we drove, the end gate snap open and a box was fall out. Ben yell and I stoped. He putted it back in and slam the end gate shut. He snag his thumb in the latch. I looked at it and rubed it. I ask if he was hurt and would of taken him to the clinic. He seem okay, but later we learn his thumb was broken.

THE PRINCIPAL PARTS OF VERBS

Verbs have four principal parts, or fundamental forms: present, present participle, past, and past participle. These principal parts tell readers when the action happened.

- **Present:** the form of the verb that would complete the sentence, "Now, we _____," or "Today, I _____." This form of the verb describes action happening now.

  Now, we eat.

  Today, I nail the plywood onto the frame.

  If we score two more points, we win the game.

- **Present participle:** the *ing* form of the verb, used with the helping verbs *is, am, are.* This verb form will complete these sentences: "I am _____," "S/he is _____," "They are _____." This form of the verb also describes action happening now. It is different from the present form because it has an *ing* ending and because a helping verb comes before it.

  Now, I am listing all of our responsibilities.

  She is grilling the burgers outside.

  We are watching the movie upstairs.

- **Past:** the form of the verb that would complete the sentence, "Yesterday, I _____," or "Yesterday, we _____." This form of the verb describes action that happened in the past.

  We followed the instructions carefully.

  Sue resigned because she objected to the new policy change.

  James snored all through lunch.

- **Past participle:** the form of the verb that would complete the sentence, "Often, I have _____," or "Often, we have _____." This form of the verb also describes action that happened in the past.

A verb is a past participle if it is used with a helping verb such as *have, has,* or *had.*

> The neighbors have returned our lawn mower.
>
> Payroll has deducted the cost of health insurance from my last check.
>
> The teenagers have consumed every speck of food in the house.

REGULAR VERBS

Regular verbs follow a standard set of rules for forming their present participle and past forms. The present participle is formed by adding *ing.* If the verb ends with the letter *e,* drop the *e* before adding *ing.* The past is formed by adding *ed.* If the verb ends with the letter *e,* just add *d.*

> *link:* present form
>
> *linking:* forms the present participle by adding *ing*
>
> *linked:* forms the past and past participle by adding *ed*
>
> *prepare:* present form
>
> *preparing:* forms the present participle by dropping the *e* and adding *ing.*
>
> *prepared:* forms the past and past participle by adding *d.*

Below is a list of twenty regular verbs and all four of their principal parts.

Present	Present Participle	Past	Past Participle
connect	connecting	connected	connected
elect	electing	elected	elected
exercise	exercising	exercised	exercised
follow	following	followed	followed
guarantee	guaranteeing	guaranteed	guaranteed
hire	hiring	hired	hired
imagine	imagining	imagined	imagined
knock	knocked	knocking	knocked
learn	learning	learned	learned
match	matching	matched	matched
notice	noticing	noticed	noticed

Present	Present Participle	Past	Past Participle
progress	progressing	progressed	progressed
rate	rating	rated	rated
salt	salting	salted	salted
solve	solving	solved	solved
target	targeting	targeted	targeted
time	timing	timed	timed
view	viewing	viewed	viewed
wash	washing	washed	washed
yell	yelling	yelled	yelled

Practice

Fill in the correct form of the verb in each of the following sentences. The present form of the verb comes at the beginning of each sentence. Check your work with the answers at the end of the chapter.

1. define   Paul _____ the word *impetus* for us.
2. leak   Water is _____ through the roof.
3. melt   The snow _____ early this year.
4. organize   Kay and Sandy are _____ the retirement dinner this year.
5. place   The custodian _____ an air freshener in the lounge.

REGULAR VERBS ENDING WITH A VOWEL AND CONSONANT

The English language has two kinds of letters: vowels and consonants. The vowels are *a, e, i, o, u*. All other letters are consonants. The letter *y*, however, sometimes works as a vowel and sometimes as a consonant.

When a verb ends with a vowel and consonant (*blot, flip, occur*), the last consonant is doubled before adding *ing* or *ed*. The table on the next page shows ten words that end this way. Look carefully at how the present participle and past forms are made.

     net: present form

     netting: forms the present participle by doubling the *t* before adding *ing*

     netted: forms the past and past participle by doubling the *t* and adding *ed trip:* present form

tripping: forms the present participle by doubling the *p* before adding *ing*

tripped: forms the past and past participle by doubling the *p* and adding *ed*

Present	Present Participle	Past	Past Participle
cap	capping	capped	capped
dab	dabbing	dabbed	dabbed
grab	grabbing	grabbed	grabbed
emit	emitting	emitted	emitted
occur	occurring	occurred	occurred
pin	pinning	pinned	pinned
scar	scarring	scarred	scarred
ship	shipping	shipped	shipped
step	stepping	stepped	stepped
trap	trapping	trapped	trapped

This rule has one exception. If the final consonant is a *w,* it is not doubled before adding *ing* or *ed.* Look at the following examples.

show: present form

showing: present participle

showed: past and past participle

sew: present form

sewing: present participle

sewed: past and past participle

Practice

Fill in the correct form of the verb in each of the following sentences. The present form of the verb comes at the beginning of each sentence. Check your work with the answers at the end of the chapter.

6. fit   My new shoes _____ my feet just fine.

7. map   The survey crew is _____ the plot this afternoon.

8. slow   Lyle _____ down as he approached the stop sign.

9. refer   I think he is _____ to the article in this morning's
paper.

10. transfer   Marcia and Peg have _____ to the new location.

REGULAR VERBS ENDING WITH A CONSONANT AND Y

When a verb ends with a consonant and *y* (*cry, empty, hurry*), the present participle is formed by adding *ing*. To create the past form, drop the *y*, replace it with *i*, and add *ed*. The examples show how this is done. The table below contains ten words that end in this way. Look carefully at how the past and past participles are formed.

> *fry:* present form
> *frying:* present participle
> *fried:* forms the past and past participle by changing the *y* to *i* and
>   adding *ed*

> *study:* present form
> *studying:* present participle
> *studied:* forms the past and past participle by changing the *y* to *i*
>   and adding *ed*

Present	Present Participle	Past	Past Participle
falsify	falsifying	falsified	falsified
magnify	magnifying	magnified	magnified
marry	marrying	married	married
multiply	multiplying	multiplied	multiplied
occupy	occupying	occupied	occupied
pity	pitying	pitied	pitied
pry	prying	pried	pried
qualify	qualifying	qualified	qualified
unify	unifying	unified	unified
verify	verifying	verified	verified

Practice

Fill in the correct form of the verb in each of the following sentences. The present form of the verb comes at the beginning of each sentence. Check your work with the answers at the end of the chapter.

11. try   The wolf _____ desperately to escape from the trap.

12. nullify   The new contract _____ the old one.

13. tally   The election committee is _____ the votes right now.

14. pity   The children _____ the caged puppy.

15. qualify Marge's time in the race _____ her for the national meet.

ONE-PART REGULAR VERBS

Some verbs in the English language have the same present, past, and past participle form. The only time these verbs change is when *ing* is added to form the present participle. Here is a partial list of those verbs, followed by several examples.

bet	hit	set
bid	hurt	shut
burst	put	spread
cost	quit	upset
cut	read	

The first baseman hit a home run. (present)

In yesterday's game, the first baseman hit a home run. (past)

The first baseman has hit twenty home runs so far this year. (past participle)

The first baseman is hitting yet another home run. (present participle—the only one that changes)

DON'T FORGET THE *ED*

Some words are written incorrectly because we don't always use or hear the *ed* in spoken English. Remember to add *ed* to the past and past participle forms of these words. The ones most commonly misused are shown in the table on the next page.

Present	Present Participle	Past	Past Participle
ask	asking	asked	asked
risk	risking	risked	risked
suppose	supposing	supposed	supposed
use	using	used	used

We asked [not *ask*] to see the record book.

The rescuers risked [not *risk*] their lives to save the stranded mountain climbers.

We are supposed [not *suppose*] to finish this for tomorrow.

This group is used [not *use*] to working together.

Don't Use *Of* in Place of *Have*

Another problem that comes up because of pronunciation is using *of* instead of *have* in participial phrases. *Could've* sounds just like *could of*—but *could have* is correct and *could of* is wrong.

Wrong: Hansel could **of** seen the danger if he had looked more carefully.

Correct: Hansel could **have** seen the danger if he had looked more carefully.

Wrong: The farmer should **of** warned us about the dog.

Correct: The farmer should **have** warned us about the dog.

Wrong: I wish the contractor would **of** taken care of this for us.

Correct: I wish the contractor would **have** taken care of this for us.

Practice

Use what you have learned about verbs to correct the following sentences. Check your work with the corrected sentences at the end of the chapter.

16. Sally wish her husband would of remembered to pack her lunch.

17. That's not the way we use to do it.

18. Juwon risk serious injury by wipe the acid spill.

19. You could of improved your chances by preparing ahead of time.

20. Ryan ask the question that the rest of us were afraid to ask.

Review

Remember the paragraph at the beginning of the chapter? Take another look at it and correct all of the errors you find. Compare your version to the corrected version below. The changes have been highlighted for you.

Ben had an accident today. He and I were haul**ing** a load of furniture from the warehouse. As we drove, the end gate snapp**ed** open and a box was fall**ing** out. Ben yell**ed** and I stopp**ed**. He **put** it back in and slamm**ed** the end gate shut. He snag**ged** his thumb in the latch. I looked at it and rub**bed** it. I asked if he was hurt and would **have** taken him to the clinic. He seem**ed** okay, but later we learn**ed** his thumb was broken.

Answers

1. defined
2. leaking
3. melted
4. organizing
5. placed
6. fit
7. mapping
8. slowed
9. referring
10. transferred
11. tried
12. nullified (or nullifies)
13. tallying
14. pitied
15. qualified
16. Sally wished her husband would have remembered to pack her lunch.
17. That's not the way we used to do it.
18. Juwon risked serious injury by wiping the acid spill.
19. You could have improved your chances by preparing ahead of time.
20. Ryan asked the question that the rest of us were afraid to ask.

CHAPTER 13

The last chapter explained how and when to use regular verbs. This chapter explains how to use irregular verbs—the ones that don't behave the way you expect a verb to act.

VERBS THAT WON'T BEHAVE

Most verbs in the English language are regular, but about 150 verbs are not. Most of the irregularities involve the ways in which the past and past participle are formed. This chapter covers many of these verbs and provides practice in using them. Read the note below, written by an employee to a supervisor. How many errors in using irregular verbs can you spot?

I done what you ask this morning. I digged through the recycling bin to look for your records. I seen a few things that seemed like what we was looking for, but I think last night's trash must have went to the dumpster, and I ain't digging in there.

IRREGULAR VERBS WITH SIMILAR PAST AND PAST PARTICIPLE FORMS

This table includes some of the most commonly used irregular verbs. All of them have the same past and past participle, except for the last three. The last three words form their principal parts in the same way and have a past participle form that is similar, though not identical, to the past form. After the table are some exercises in using these verbs.

Present	Past	Past Participle (used with *have, has, had*)
bite	bit	bit
dig	dug	dug
bleed	bled	bled
hear	heard	heard
hold	held	held
light	lit	lit
meet	met	met
pay	paid	paid
say	said	said
sell	sold	sold
tell	told	told
shine	shone	shone
shoot	shot	shot
sit	sat	sat
spin	spun	spun
spit	spat	spat
win	won	won
swear	swore	sworn
tear	tore	torn
wear	wore	worn

Practice

Choose the correct form of the verb in each of the sentences below. Remember to use present tense for things happening now, and past tense for things that have already happened. Check your work with the answers at the end of the chapter.

   1. The dentist (ask, asked) me to (bite, bit) down hard on the X-ray tabs.

2. Head wounds (bleed, bled) freely.

3. I (hear, heard) yesterday that you plan to move before summer.

4. Will (pay, paid) his bills with a credit card.

5. It's cold enough to (light, lit) the furnace.

6. Breanna never (tell, told) us what you meant.

7. The moon (shine, shone) through the trees, making eerie shadows on the ground.

8. The tires did nothing but (spin, spun) on the glare ice.

9. If we (win, won) this game, we advance to the playoffs.

10. Collin (tear, tore) his jeans climbing over the barbed wire fence.

MORE IRREGULAR VERBS WITH TWO IDENTICAL PARTS

Here's another table of irregular verbs whose past and past participle are the same. Study them, and then try your hand at the exercises.

Present	Past	Past Participle (used with *have, has, had*)
creep	crept	crept
deal	dealt	dealt
keep	kept	kept
kneel	knelt	knelt
leave	left	left
mean	meant	meant
send	sent	sent
sleep	slept	slept
spend	spent	spent
sweep	swept	swept
bring	brought	brought
buy	bought	bought
catch	caught	caught
fight	fought	fought
teach	taught	taught
think	thought	thought
feed	fed	fed
flee	fled	fled
find	found	found
grind	ground	ground

Practice

Choose the correct form of the verb in each of the sentences below. Remember to use present tense for things happening now, and past tense for things that have already happened. Check your work with the answers at the end of the chapter.

11. The gambler folded the hand he was (deal, dealt).
12. The detectives (keep, kept) the suspect under surveillance all last night.
13. The would-be knight (kneel, knelt) before the king.
14. Do you (mean, meant) that we'll be without electricity all evening?
15. The twins (spend, spent) last evening with their grandparents.
16. We always (bring, brought) deviled eggs to every family picnic.
17. The center fielder (catch, caught) the ball and threw it to home plate.
18. Hal (think, thought) the fruit would have been delivered by now.
19. We (find, found) water in our basement every spring.
20. The burglars (flee, fled) on foot after they left the convenience store.

IRREGULAR VERBS WITH THREE DISTINCT FORMS

The irregular verbs in the table below are grouped with other verbs that form their principal parts in similar ways. See if you can detect any patterns or groups in these irregular verbs.

Present	Past	Past Participle (used with *have, has, had*)
begin	began	begun
ring	rang	rung
sing	sang	sung
spring	sprang	sprung
do	did	done
go	went	gone
am	was	been
is	was	been
drink	drank	drunk
shrink	shrank	shrunk

Present	Past	Past Participle (used with *have, has, had*)
sink	sank	sunk
stink	stank	stunk
blow	blew	blown
draw	drew	drawn
grow	grew	grown
know	knew	known
throw	threw	thrown
fly	flew	flown
drive	drove	driven
strive	strove	striven

Practice

Choose the correct form of the verb in each of the sentences below. Remember to use present tense for things happening now, past tense for things that have already happened, and past participle with *have, has,* or *had.* Check your work with the answers at the end of the chapter.

21. It has (begin, began, begun) to rain.
22. The congregation (sing, sang, sung) the first two verses of the hymn.
23. The builder (do, did, done) all the planning for us.
24. The neighbors have (go, went, gone) on vacation.
25. Jack (is, was, has been) putting in overtime for that last three weeks.
26. The sweatshirt (shrink, shrank, shrunk) when I washed it.
27. The ship must have (sink, sank, sunk) about 125 years ago.
28. All of their children have (grow, grew, grown) up and moved away.
29. The proprietor (know, knew, known) his supplies were running short.
30. The teenage boy (drive, drove, driven) his way to high insurance rates.

MORE THREE-PART IRREGULAR VERBS

The table on the next page also includes verbs grouped with others that form their principal parts in similar ways. See if you can detect the patterns.

Present	Past	Past Participle (used with *have, has, had*)
choose	chose	chosen
rise	rose	risen
break	broke	broken
speak	spoke	spoken
fall	fell	fallen
shake	shook	shaken
take	took	taken
forget	forgot	forgotten
get	got	gotten
give	gave	given
forgive	forgave	forgiven
forsake	forsook	forsaken
hide	hid	hidden
ride	rode	ridden
write	wrote	written
come	came	come
overcome	overcame	overcome
run	ran	run
freeze	froze	frozen
steal	stole	stolen

Practice

Choose the correct form of the verb in each of the sentences below. Remember to use present tense for things happening now, past tense for things that have already happened, and past participle with *have, has,* or *had.* Check your work with the answers at the end of the chapter.

31. The gambler must have (choose, chose, chosen) the lucky dice.

32. The band on this watch (break, broke, broken).

33. Hoards of walnuts (fall, fell, fallen) from the tree that fall.

34. The audience grew deathly quiet when they realized the star had (forget, forgot, forgotten) his lines.

35. Becky's parents (give, gave, given) her sponges for Christmas.

36. The dog must have (hide, hid, hidden) your slippers.

37. Have you (write, wrote, written) to your mother lately?

38. The newlyweds (come, came) home to a completely empty house.

39. Water will (freeze, froze, frozen) at 32 degrees Fahrenheit.

40. More time has been (steal, stole, stolen) by procrastination than any other thief.

AIN'T

Ain't is a substandard English word that should never be used in business language. It belongs in the same category as *wanna* and *gonna*. You may hear these words when people speak, but they are not used in formal writing. Instead of *ain't,* use *is not* or *isn't, am not,* and *are not* or *aren't.*

Incorrect: I ain't interested in your product.
Correct: I am not interested in your product.

Incorrect: He ain't the problem here.
Correct: He isn't the problem here.

Incorrect: We ain't supposed to know about the party.
Correct: We aren't supposed to know about the party.

Review

Remember the paragraph at the beginning of the chapter? Take another look at it and correct all of the verb errors you find. Compare your version of the paragraph to the corrected one below. The changes have been highlighted for you.

> I **did** what you asked this morning. I **dug** through the recycling bin to look for your records. I **saw** a few things that seemed like what we **were** looking for, but I think last night's trash must have **gone** to the dumpster, and I'**m not** digging in there.

Choose the correct form of the verb in each of the following sentences. Check your work with the answers at the end of the chapter.

41. Your department certainly (do, did, done) a good job on this project.

42. The manager just (throw, threw, thrown) away a chance to increase the store's sales.

43. The president (speak, spoke, spoken) at the cabinet meeting.

44. The phone has (ring, rang, rung) continuously all day long.
45. The minister (come, came) to the point very early in the sermon.
46. Harriet (see, saw, seen) the advertising for the new product in a catalog.
47. The new tree has not yet (begin, began, begun) to produce fruit.
48. Has the admitting staff (go, went, gone) nuts?
49. Heather lost a filling when she (bite, bit, bitten) into the piece of hard candy.
50. The attendant couldn't believe that someone had actually (steal, stole, stolen) a car from the ramp.

Answers

1. asked, bite	18. thought	35. gave
2. bleed	19. find	36. hidden
3. heard	20. fled	37. written
4. paid	21. begun	38. came
5. light	22. sang	39. freeze
6. told	23. did	40. stolen
7. shone	24. gone	41. did
8. spin	25. has been	42. threw
9. win	26. shrank	43. spoke
10. tore	27. sunk	44. rung
11. dealt	28. grown	45. came
12. kept	29. knew	46. saw
13. knelt	30. drove	47. begun
14. mean	31. chosen	48. gone
15. spent	32. broke	49. bit
16. bring	33. fell	50. stolen
17. caught	34. forgotten	

CHAPTER | 14

Yesterday, today, and tomorrow: This chapter covers the fine points of verb tenses, the verb forms that express the time of an action. By the end of this chapter you'll have a better understanding of how to use past-, present-, and future-tense verbs.

DON'T BE TENSE ABOUT VERBS

Tense gives readers clues about time, so writers need to know how to use it accurately. This chapter explains how to keep verb tense consistent and when to switch tense.

KEEPING VERB TENSE CONSISTENT

The tense of a verb tells when an action occurs, occurred, or will occur. Verbs have three basic tenses: present, past, and future. A passage that begins in present tense should continue in present tense. If it begins in past tense, it should stay in past tense. Do not mix tenses as you write.

Wrong: The officer **unlocked** the trunk and **searches** for contraband.
Correct: The officer **unlocked** the trunk and **searched** for contraband.
Correct: The officer **unlocks** the trunk and **searches** for contraband.

Wrong: When we **increase** advertising expense, we **reduced** profits.
Correct: When we **increase** advertising expense, we **reduce** profits.
Correct: When we **increased** advertising expense, we **reduced** profits.

USING TENSE TO CONVEY MEANING

Using verb tense carefully helps writers avoid the confusion. The examples below illustrate how tense can completely change the meaning of a sentence.

Richard discovered that Patty had left home and gone to work. (Patty went to work.)
Richard discovered that Patty had left home and went to work. (Richard went to work.)

Linda told the officer that she had answered the door and got a glass of wine. (Linda got the wine near the time she was talking to the officer.)
Linda told the officer that she had answered the door and had gotten a glass of wine. (Linda got the wine after she answered the door.)

THE FINE POINTS OF VERB TENSE

Sometimes a writer must show that an action occurred at another time, regardless of the tense in which the passage was begun. To allow this, each of the three basic tenses has three subdivisions: progressive, perfect, and progressive perfect.

Present tense shows action that happens now or action that happens routinely. The **present progressive** tense shows an action that is happening now. A helping, or auxiliary, verb (*am, is,* or *are*) precedes the *ing* form (progressive form) of the verb. The **present perfect** tense shows an action that began in the past. A helping verb (*have* or *has*) precedes the past form of the verb. The **present perfect progressive** tense also shows action that began in the past and is continuing in the present. Helping verbs (*have been* or *has been*) precede the verb written in its *ing* form (progressive form).

Present (shows action happening now)	Progressive (*ing* form preceded by *am, is, are*)	Perfect (shows action that began in the past; uses *has, have*)	Perfect Progressive (shows action that began in the past and continues now; uses *has* or *have been*)
Optimists hope for the best.	Optimists are hoping for the best.	Optimists have hoped for the best.	Optimists have been hoping for the best.
Smoking causes cancer.	Smoking is causing cancer.	Smoking has caused cancer.	Smoking has been causing cancer.

All present-tense forms can be used without shifting verb tense. Look at the paragraph below to see how this is done. The verbs are italicized, and the words in parentheses identify the tense.

> The city planners *are hoping* (present progressive) to revamp the old stadium, which the Redbirds *use* (present). For years fans *have complained* (present perfect) about parking, and officials *pay* (present) little attention. Season ticket holders *have been boycotting* (present perfect progressive) games for the last month, but their absence *has gone* (present perfect) unnoticed. They *demand* (present) adequate parking.

Past tense shows action that happened in the past. It uses the past form of the verb. The **past progressive** tense shows a continuing action in the past. A helping verb (*was* or *were*) precedes the progressive form of the verb. The **past perfect** tense shows an action completed in the past or completed before some other past action. The helping verb *had* precedes the past participle form of the verb. The **past perfect progressive** tense shows continuing action that began in the past. The helping verbs *had been* precede the progressive form of the verb.

Past (action occurred in the past) Parents spoke to the teachers.	Progressive (*ing* form, continuing action in the past; uses *was, were*)	Perfect (action completed prior to another action; uses *had*)	Perfect Progressive (continuing action started in the past; uses *had been*)
	Parents were speaking to the teachers.	Parents had spoken to the teachers.	Parents had been speaking to the teachers.
A principal held the meetings.	A principal was holding the meetings.	A principal had held the meetings.	A principal had been holding the meetings.

All past-tense forms can be used in one writing passage, as they do not constitute a shift in tense. The paragraph below illustrates how this is done. The verbs are italicized, and the words in parentheses identify the tense.

Last fall, school officials *warned* (past) students about bringing pagers to school. Most students *complied* (past) with the request; however, some *ignored* (past) the rules and *continued* (past) to carry the pagers they *had been bringing* (past perfect progressive) to school. They *had carried* (past perfect) them the previous year and *planned* (past) to continue. Around mid-year, several students *were suspended* (past). A *Times* reporter, who *had been following* (past perfect progressive) the story, *challenged* (past) the legality of the school's rule. A suit *has been filed* (past perfect) on behalf of the suspended students, but it *has* not *come* (past perfect) before the court.

Future tense shows action that has yet to happen. The helping verbs *will, would,* or *shall* precede the present form of the verb. The **future progressive** tense shows continuing actions in the future. The helping-verb phrases *will be, shall be,* or *would be* precede the progressive form of the verb. The **future perfect** tense shows actions that will be completed at a certain time in the future. The helping-verb phrases *will have, would have,* or *will have been* precede the past participle form of the verb. The **future perfect progressive** tense shows continuing actions that will be completed at a certain time in the future. The verb phrases *will have been, would have been,* or *shall have been* precede the progressive form of the verb.

Future (action that will happen; uses *will, would, shall*)	Progressive (continuing action that will happen)	Perfect (action that will be completed by a certain time)	Perfect Progressive (continuing action that will be completed by a certain time)
We will begin a letter-writing campaign.	Everyone will be writing letters.	By summer, we will have written reams of letters.	Legislators will have been receiving letters throughout the year.
Newspapers will cover this case.	Newspapers will be covering this case.	By summer, every newspaper will have written about this case.	Newspapers will have been covering the case throughout the year.

All future-tense forms can be used in one writing passage, as they do not constitute a shift in tense. The paragraph below illustrates how this is done. The verbs are italicized for you, and the words in parentheses identify the tense.

Because of severe spring flooding, the city *will construct* (future) levies along the river. This *will prevent* (future) damage to the downtown area. They *will be building* (future progressive) these structures along a three-mile stretch of river. By spring, the levies *will have been built* (future perfect) and *will have been protecting* (future perfect progressive) downtown businesses from flood damage.

IMPROPER USE OF PAST TENSE

Don't use past tense to make a statement about a present condition.

Zelda saw the new director. He **was** very tall. [Isn't he still tall?]
Zelda saw the new director. He **is** very tall.

I visited a bed and breakfast inn near the edge of town. The building **was** Victorian. [Isn't it still Victorian?]
I visited a bed and breakfast inn near the edge of town. The building **is** Victorian.

PRESENT TENSE FOR STATEMENTS OF GENERAL TRUTH OR FACT

Even if a passage is written in past tense, a general statement of truth or fact is written in present tense.

> During Galileo's time few people *believed* (past) that the earth *revolves* (present) around the sun.

> The engineer *explained* (past) to the city council that the streets *run* (present) parallel to the freeway.

SUBJUNCTIVE MOOD FOR CONDITIONS CONTRARY TO FACT

When Tevya in *Fiddler on the Roof* sings, "If I were a rich man . . ." he uses the verb *were* to signal that he is only imagining what he would do as a rich man. The subjunctive mood of verbs is used to express something that is wished for or that is contrary to fact. The subjunctive of *was* is *were*.

> If you *were* a cat, you could be entirely dependent on human beings. [You are not a cat.]

> If Anthony *were* more responsible, he could be trusted with this job. [Anthony is not responsible.]

Practice

Use what you have learned about verb tense to choose the correct option in each of the following sentences. Check your work with the answers at the end of the chapter.

1. After Ethel knocked on the door, she (ring, rang, had rung) the doorbell.
2. Before I get on the plane, she will (read, have read) my parting words.
3. My teacher explained why Mars (is, was) red.
4. I would finish the job if I (was, were) you.
5. The office morale has already (begin, began, begun) to suffer.
6. The nurse (takes, took) my pulse and (measures, measured) my blood pressure.
7. Most of us wish we would (of, have) taken stock options rather than year-end bonuses.

8. Charles wishes he would have ordered a large burger because his (is, was) too small.

9. Dr. Carnes announced that the department chair (is, was) responsible for work schedules.

10. The packing plant could cut transportation costs if it (was, were) closer to a livestock confinement.

10. The customers would be happier if we (provide, would provide, provided) free refills.

11. If I (was, were) king of the United States, I'd abolish income taxes.

12. Alvin opened the door and (look, looks, looked) inside.

13. When we increase maintenance service, we (reduce, reduced) repair costs.

14. The company had dumped waste into the river for years and it (plans, planned, had planned) to continue doing so.

15. I met the new technician. He (is, was) very personable.

16. Because Peter loved his job, he (takes, took) it very seriously.

17. I ate at a new restaurant last night, and the decor (is, was) wonderful.

18. I like knowing that my work (is, was) done well.

19. Hesari must have been desperate to (take, took, have taken) time off work.

Answers

1. rang
2. have read
3. is
4. were
5. begun
6. took/measured, or takes/measures
7. have
8. is
9. is
10. were
11. would provide
12. were
13. looked
14. reduce
15. planned
16. is
17. took
18. is
19. is
20. have taken

LEARNINGEXPRESS

20 Academy Street, P.O. Box 7100, Norwalk, CT 06852-9879

To provide you with the best test prep, basic skills, and
career materials, we would appreciate your help.
Please answer the following questions and return this postage paid piece.
Thank you for your time!

Name : _____

Address : _____

_____

Age : _____ Sex : ☐ Male ☐ Female

Highest Level of School Completed : ☐ High School ☐ College

1) I am currently :

A student — Year/level: _____

Employed — Job title: _____

Other — Please explain: _____

2) Jobs/careers of interest to me are :

1. _____

2. _____

3. _____

3) If you are a student, did your guidance/career counselor provide
you with job information/materials? _____

4) What newspapers and/or magazines do you subscribe to or
read regularly? _____

_____

5) Do you own a computer? _____

If so, do you have Internet access? _____

How often do you go on-line? _____

6) The last time you visited a bookstore, did you make a purchase?

_____

Have you purchased career-related materials from bookstores?

_____

7) Do you subscribe to cable TV? _____

Which channels to you watch regularly (please give network
letters rather than channel numbers)?

_____

_____

8) Which radio stations do you listen to regularly (please give call
letters and city name)?

_____

_____

9) How did you hear about the book you just purchased from
LearningExpress?

An ad? _____

If so, where? _____

An order form in the back of another book? _____

A recommendation? _____

A bookstore? _____

Other? _____

10) Title of the book this card came from:

_____

LearningExpress books are also available in the test prep/study guide section of your local bookstore.

LEARNiNGEXPRESS

The leading publisher of customized career and test preparation books!

LearningExpress is an affiliate of Random House, Inc.

CHAPTER | 15

He don't or he doesn't?
Most native English
speakers automatically
choose the second version.
Subject-verb agreement is
so important in speaking
and writing that errors in
this area really stand out.
This chapter highlights
some of the situations
that cause agreement
problems even for native
speakers and explains
how to handle them
correctly in writing.

MAKING SUBJECTS AND VERBS AGREE

When a subject in a clause—the person or thing doing the action—matches the verb in number (both singular or both plural), we say the subject and verb are *in agreement*. Most English speakers have little trouble matching subjects with the correct verbs. A few grammatical constructions pose most of the problems. This chapter explains the concept of subject-verb agreement and provides practice in those problem areas.

The memo on the next page contains several subject-verb agreement errors. See how many you can spot. By the end of this chapter, you'll probably be able to recognize them all.

To: Jessica Amerson
From: Tyson Hall
Re: Aides/floor nurse dispute
Date: July 21, 1997

The nurses' aides was having trouble with the floor nurse yesterday. He don't think he should help with unloading supplies. Every one of the aides are just as busy as he is. The aides think he should do his part too. They wasn't very happy with him when he refused. Melinda and Connie is thinking about filing a complaint. Neither the aides nor the floor nurse need this fuss. Maybe you can see if either the floor nurse or the aides is willing to find a better solution.

MAKING SUBJECTS AGREE WITH THEIR VERBS IN NUMBER

A subject should agree with its verb in number. In other words, if a subject is singular, the verb must be singular; if the subject is plural, the verb must be plural. If you are unsure whether a verb is singular or plural, apply this simple test. Fill in the blanks in the two sentences below with the matching form of the verb. The verb form that best completes the first sentence is singular. The verb form that best completes the second sentence is plural.

He _____. [Singular]
They _____. [Plural]

Look at these examples using the verbs *look, do,* and *was.* Try it yourself with any verb that confuses you. Unlike nouns, most verbs ending in *s* are singular.

He <u>looks</u>.	He <u>does</u>.	He <u>was</u>.
They <u>look</u>.	They <u>do.</u>	They <u>were.</u>

Note, however, that the subject *I,* even though it is a single person, usually takes the plural form.

I <u>look.</u>	I <u>do.</u>	I <u>am.</u>

PROBLEM VERB FORMS AND CONSTRUCTIONS

The verb form *to be—be, am, is, are, was, were*—can pose special problems because it's so irregular. The list below shows how to use the verb form *to be*.

Subject	Present	Past	Past Participle
I	I am	I was	I have been
you	you are	you were	you have been
he, she, it	he is	she was	it has been
we	we are	we were	we have been
they	they are	they were	they have been

Never use the *be* form after a subject.

Incorrect: I be going.

Correct: I am going.

Incorrect: They be on their way.

Correct: They are on their way.

Two other constructions often cause problems for people: *doesn't/don't* (meaning *does not, do not*) and *wasn't/weren't* (meaning *was not, were not*). *Doesn't* and *wasn't* are singular; *don't* and *weren't* are plural. (But remember that *I* takes the plural form.)

I don't want to go.

She doesn't want to go.

They don't want to go.

I wasn't doing anything wrong.

You weren't doing anything wrong.

We weren't doing anything wrong.

PHRASES FOLLOWING SUBJECTS DON'T AFFECT VERBS

Pay careful attention to the subject in a sentence. Do not allow a phrase following it to mislead you into using a verb that does not agree with the subject. The subjects and verbs are highlighted in the following examples.

One of the chairs **is** damaged.

The window **designs** by Rick Baker **are** complex and colorful.

A **manual** with thorough instructions **comes** with this printer.

The **principal**, along with her three associates, **returns** from the workshop today.

SPECIAL SINGULAR SUBJECTS

Some nouns are singular even though they end in *s*. Despite the plural form, they require a singular verb because we think of them as a single thing. Most of the nouns in the following list are singular. Some can be either singular or plural, depending on their use in the sentence. These are just a few examples: *measles, mumps, news, checkers* or *marbles* (games), *physics, economics, mathematics, civics, athletics, sports, politics, statistics.*

> The **news is** over at 9:30.
>
> **Darts is** my favorite game.
>
> **Sports is** a healthy stress reliever. Low-impact **aerobics is** best for older adults.

Words stating a single amount or a time require a singular verb. Examine a sentence carefully to see if the amount or time is considered a single measure.

> Two dollars **is** the price of a hamburger. (single amount)
>
> Two dollars **are** lying on the table.
>
> Three hours **was** required to assemble this machine. (single measure)
>
> Three hours of each day **were** used for planning.
>
> Three-quarters of her time **is** spent working.

Practice

Circle the correct verb in each of the following sentences.

1. If the boss (jokes, joke), we (laughs, laugh).
2. A single tree now (grows, grow) where the forest used to (grows, grow).
3. Constella (speaks, speak) English, but her parents (speaks, speak) Spanish.
4. The clerk (rings, ring) up the sales while the customers (waits, wait) in line.
5. The carolers (hums, hum) while the soloist (sings, sing)
6. The bright walls (doesn't, don't) seem very relaxing.
7. The shipment (wasn't, weren't) here when we arrived this morning.
8. The bank (doesn't, don't) open until 9:30 on Saturday mornings.
9. Mabel couldn't drive to work because her car (wasn't, weren't) starting.

10. Paula (doesn't, don't) think the files (is, are) in storage.

11. One of the secretaries (is, are) finishing the newsletter that (was, were) scheduled to go out last week.

12. The petty cash box, along with the receipts, (is, are) turned in at the end of the day.

13. These statistics (is, are) the result of careful research.

14. Statistics (was, were) my most difficult math course in high school.

15. Half of the sandwich (was, were) eaten.

16. Half of the sandwiches (was, were) tuna salad.

MAKING PRONOUN SUBJECTS MATCH THEIR VERBS IN NUMBER

A pronoun is a word that takes the place of a noun. For example, in this sentence, "All of the cookies were decorated," the word *all* stands for or refers to cookies.

Pronouns used as subjects present a problem for even the most sophisticated speakers of English. Some pronouns are always plural. Other pronouns are always singular. Some of these are also called *indefinite* pronouns because they refer to no specific person of thing. A handful of pronouns can be either singular or plural.

SINGULAR PRONOUNS

These pronouns are always singular. They require singular verbs.

each	anyone	nobody
either	everybody	one
neither	everyone	somebody
anybody	no one	someone

See how these pronouns take singular verbs in the following examples:

Someone **left** a pocketbook in the cloakroom.

Has *anybody* seen my pocketbook?

Everyone **wants** to know where my pocketbook is.

Nobody **has** seen it.

Each, either, and *neither* are the pronouns most likely to be misused. You can avoid a mismatch by mentally replacing the other words between the pronoun and the verb with the word *one*. Look at the following examples to see how this is done.

Each of the boys wants his own car.
Each *one* **wants** his own car.

Either of the associates knows where the records are kept.
Either *one* **knows** where the records are kept.

These sentences may sound awkward. So many speakers misuse these pronouns that you may have become accustomed to hearing them used incorrectly. Despite that, the substitution trick (*one* for the words following the pronoun) will help you avoid this mistake.

For questions beginning with *has* or *have*, remember that *has* is singular while *have* is plural. Pay special attention to the verb-subject combination in a question. In fact, the correct verb is easier to identify if you turn the question into a statement.

(Is, Are) some of the advertisers noticing the difference?
Some of the advertisers **are** noticing the difference.

(Has, Have) either of the inspectors filed a report?
Either *one* **has** filed a report.

(Does, Do) each of the trucks have a hoist?
Each *one* **does** have a hoist.

PLURAL PRONOUNS

These pronouns are always plural and require a plural verb:

both   many
few   several

SINGULAR/PLURAL PRONOUNS

The following pronouns can be either singular or plural:

all   none
any   some
most

The words following these pronouns determine whether the verbs are singular or plural. If the phrase following the pronoun contains a plural noun or pronoun, the verb must be plural. If the phrase following the pronoun contains a singular noun or pronoun, the verb must be singular. See how this is done in the sentences below. The key words are highlighted.

Singular	Plural
All of the **work is** planned.	**All** of the **jobs are** planned.
Is any of the **pie** remaining?	**Are any** of the **pieces** of pie remaining?
Most of the **milk was** sour.	**Most** of the **glasses** of milk **were** sour.
None of the **time was** spent very well.	**None** of the **hours were** spent very well.
Some of the **fruit was** shipped.	**Some** of the **apples were** shipped.

Practice

Practice matching pronoun subjects with verbs by circling the correct verb in each of the following sentences.

17. None of these keys (unlocks, unlock) the back door.
18. Each of the project components (takes, take) several hours to complete.
19. All of the box lunches (has, have) been given away.
20. Some of the animals (was, were) moved for the winter.
21. Either of these paintings (is, are) is perfect for my house.
22. (Was, Were) any of the cables long enough?
23. (Do, Does) each of the keyboards have a built-in wrist support?
24. (Has, Have) either of the tenants paid the rent?
25. Neither of our fleet vehicles (needs, need) to be serviced.
26. Both of the trainees (seems, seem) motivated.
27. A friend at one of my jobs also (works, work) for the city.
28. None of our problems (goes, go) unnoticed by the regular customers.
29. An exercise program (helps, help) your frame of mind.
30. Each of these decongestants (causes, cause) drowsiness.

COMPOUND SUBJECTS

Compound subjects, which are those joined by *and, or,* or *not,* need special attention.

SINGULAR SUBJECTS JOINED BY *AND*

If two nouns or pronouns are joined by *and,* they require a plural verb.

> He and she **want** to take a vacation.
>
> Jack and Jill **insist** on finding a flat prairie on which to walk.

SINGULAR SUBJECTS JOINED BY *OR* OR *NOR*

If two singular nouns or pronouns are joined by *or* or *nor,* they require a singular verb. Think of them as two separate sentences and you'll never make a mistake in agreement.

> Art or Elaine **wants** to get a new car.
>
> Art **wants** to get a new car.
>
> Elaine **wants** to get a new car.

SINGULAR AND PLURAL SUBJECTS JOINED BY *OR* OR *NOR*

Singular and plural subjects joined by *or* or *nor* require a verb that agrees with the subject closest to the verb.

> Neither coach nor the **players like** the lineup.
>
> Neither the players nor the **coach likes** the lineup.

VERBS AGREE WITH SUBJECTS, NOT THE WORD FOLLOWING THE VERB

Take care not to let the words following the verb confuse you about the real subject of the sentence.

> **Taxes were** the biggest issue in the campaign.
>
> The biggest **issue** in the campaign **was** taxes.

> A serious **problem** for corn growers **is** weeds.
>
> **Weeds are** a serious problem for corn growers.

WHEN THE SUBJECT FOLLOWS THE VERB

When a sentence asks a question or begins with the word *there* or *here,* the subject follows the verb. Locate the subject of the sentence and make certain the verb matches it. In the example sentences below, the subjects and verbs are highlighted in the correct sentences.

Wrong	Correct
What is the terms of the agreement?	What **are** the **terms** of the agreement?
Why is his words garbled?	Why **are** his **words** garbled?
Here's the statistics they compiled.	Here **are** the **statistics** they compiled.
There is six sackers asking for help.	There **are** six **sackers** asking for help.

Inverted sentences also contain a subject that follows, rather than precedes, a verb. Locate the subject in an inverted sentence and make certain the verb agrees with it. In the example sentences below, the subjects and verbs in the corrected sentences are highlighted.

Wrong	Correct
Inside your drawer is the documents I finished.	Inside your drawer **are** the **documents** I finished.
Out of nowhere comes three new accounts.	Out of nowhere **come** three new **accounts**.
Up in the stands go the fan who spilled my drink.	Up in the stands **goes** the **fan** who spilled my drink.

Practice

Practice what you have learned about matching verbs and subjects by choosing the correct verb in each of the following sentences. Check your work with the answers at the end of the chapter.

31. Every other day either Oscar or Lorraine (takes, take) the car to town.
32. Neither the sound nor the rhythm (matches, match) the other stanzas in the poem.
33. Either the employees or the manager (orders, order) the inventory reduction.
34. Either the manager or the employees (orders, order) the inventory reduction.
35. (Is, Are) the children's department on this floor?

36. My daughter's passion (is, are) crafts.

37. (Was, Were) there any two-piece suits left on the rack?

38. There (isn't, aren't) many weeks left before summer.

39. Here (is, are) the data we needed.

40. Off into the sunset (runs, run) the herd of mustangs.

Review

Remember the memo at the beginning of the chapter? Go back and try to correct it, then compare your version to the corrected one below. The changes are highlighted.

To: Jessica Amerson
From: Tyson Hall
Re: Aides/floor nurse dispute
Date: July 21, 1997

The nurses' aides **were** having trouble with the floor nurse yesterday. He **doesn't** think he should help with unloading supplies. Every one of the aides **is** just as busy as he is. The aides think he should do his part too. They **weren't** very happy with him when he refused. Melinda and Connie **are** thinking about filing a complaint. Neither the aides nor the floor nurse **needs** this fuss. Maybe you can see if either the floor nurse or the aides **are** willing to find a better solution.

Answers

1. jokes, laugh
2. grows, grow
3. speaks, speak
4. rings, wait
5. hum, sings
6. don't
7. wasn't
8. doesn't
9. wasn't
10. doesn't, are
11. is, was
12. is
13. are
14. was
15. was
16. were
17. unlock
18. takes
19. have
20. were
21. is
22. Were
23. Does
24. Has
25. needs
26. seem
27. works
28. go
29. helps
30. causes
31. takes
32. matches
33. orders
34. order
35. Is
36. is
37. Were
38. aren't
39. is
40. runs

CHAPTER | 16

Using the right pronouns in sentences can be tricky. Pronouns are misused so often in speech that few people really know how to avoid pronoun errors in writing. This chapter shows you a few tricks for getting the pronouns right every time.

BEATING THE PRONOUN ODDS

Like verbs, pronouns that are misused in writing can confuse the reader. This chapter explains the basic principles of pronoun use and highlights the most common pronoun problems: agreement, incomplete constructions, reflexive pronouns, and ambiguous pronoun references.

PRONOUNS AND ANTECEDENTS

A pronoun is a word that takes the place of a noun or another pronoun. The noun represented by a pronoun is called its **antecedent**. The word *ante* means "before," and *cede* means "come." So the literal meaning of *antecedent* is "comes before." Usually, the antecedent comes before the pronoun in a sentence. In the following example sentences, the pronouns are italicized and the antecedents (the nouns they represent) are underlined.

The state <u>employees</u> received *their* benefits.

<u>Erica</u> thought *she* saw the stolen <u>van</u> and reported *it* to the authorities.

The floor <u>manager</u> hates these <u>overstocks</u> because *he* knows *they* reduce profits.

INDEFINITE PRONOUN ANTECEDENTS

A pronoun must match the number of its antecedent. In other words, if the antecedent is singular, the pronoun must be singular; if the antecedent is plural, the pronoun must be plural.

People usually don't make mistakes when matching a pronoun with a noun antecedent. However, sometimes a pronoun represents another pronoun. In the last chapter you learned about singular pronouns. These words are also known as **indefinite pronouns,** because they don't refer to one specific person of thing. The antecedents of singular, or indefinite pronouns require singular pronouns. Here is the list again.

each	anyone	nobody
either	everybody	one
neither	everyone	somebody
anybody	no one	someone

A pronoun with one of the words from this list as its antecedent must be singular. In the example sentences below, the antecent is underlined and the pronouns are italicized.

<u>Each</u> (singular) of the women wore *her* (singular) favorite outfit to the ball.

<u>Anyone</u> (singular) who enters the steer wrestling should pay up *his* (singular) life insurance.

<u>Someone</u> left *her* makeup in the rest room.

<u>Neither</u> of the tenants could find *his* (or *her*) copy of the lease.

- If two or more singular nouns or pronouns are joined by *and*, use a plural pronoun.

  <u>Bill Gates and Sam Walton</u> built *their* empires from scratch.

  If <u>he and she</u> need this information, *they* should ask me.

When Grandma and Grandpa come to visit, *they* always bring food.

- If two or more singular nouns or pronouns are joined by *or*, use a singular pronoun.

     <u>Trent or Jared </u>will loan you *his* car for this errand.

     The <u>lion or the tiger</u> will complete *its* act.

     Remember to give <u>Jane or Rita</u> *her* appointment card.

- If a singular and a plural noun or pronoun are joined by *or*, the pronoun agrees with the closest noun or pronoun it represents.

     Neither the students nor the <u>teacher</u> (singular) brought *his* (singular) book to class.

     Neither the teacher not the <u>students</u> (plural) brought *their* (plural) books to class.

Practice

Choose the correct pronoun in each of the following sentences. Check your work with the answers at the end of the chapter.

1. No one in (her, their) right mind would follow your advice.
2. Neither the soldiers nor the sergeant was sure of (his, their) location.
3. Anyone who is interested in the pilot project should sign (his, their) name on this contract.
4. Ask someone in maintenance to fix this desk, and (he, they) probably will take care of it right away.
5. Neither Gary nor Willie will inconvenience (himself, themselves) to cover your mistake.
6. If you shear a pin on this motor, (it, they) is hard to repair.
7. Ray knows someone who might give you (her, their) old dorm refrigerator.
8. Almost anybody can improve (his, their) writing by using *Grammar Essentials.*
9. If you're interested in pleasing customers, don't make (her, them) wait.
10. Arnold or Jacques will bring (his, their) recorder so (he, they) can tape the interview.

PRONOUNS AS SUBJECTS AND OBJECTS

A single pronoun in a sentence is easy to use correctly. In fact, most English speakers would readily identify the mistakes in the following sentences.

Me worked on the project with **he**.

Diane gave **she** a lift home.

Most people know that *Me* in the first sentence should be *I* and that *he* should be *him*. They would also know that *she* in the second sentence should be *her*. Such errors are easy to spot when the pronouns are used alone in a sentence. The problem occurs when a pronoun is used with a noun or another pronoun. See if you can spot the error in this sentence.

The new machinist worked with Kirsten and I.

In the sentence above, the word *I* should be *me*. If you turn the sentence into two separate sentences, the error becomes very obvious.

The new machinist worked with Kirsten.

The new machinist worked with me [not *I*].

Try to spot the errors in these three sentences.

The officer spoke to my sister and I.

Natalie and me are going to the theater.

The new owner gave he and I a different assignment.

- In the first sentence, *I* should be *me*.

     The officer spoke to my sister.

     The officer spoke to me [not *I*].

- In the second sentence, *me* should be *I*. You must change the plural verb *are* to *is* and *am* when you think of the sentences separately.

     Natalie is going to the theater.

     I [not *me*] am going to the theater.

- In the third sentence, *he* and *I* should be *him* and *me*.

     The new owner gave him [not *he*] a different assignment.

     The new owner gave me [not *I*] a different assignment.

Splitting a sentence in two does not work as well with the preposition *between*. If you substitute *with* for *between*, then the error is easier to spot.

The disagreement is between (she, her) and (I, me).

The disagreement is with her. (not *she*)

The disagreement is with me. (not *I*)

Practice

Choose the correct pronoun in the following sentences. Check your work with the answers at the end of the chapter.

11. Bonnie and (he, him) saw the show with Bernard and (I, me).
12. Neither my children nor my husband knows what (he, they) will get me for Christmas.
13. Christine and (I, me) always clean up the lounge.
14. The conductor let (he, him) and (I, me) into the club car.
15. Did you heard the latest news about (she, her) and (they, them)?
16. Melissa and (I, me) both witnessed the accident.

NOUN-PRONOUN PAIRS

Sometimes a noun in a sentence is immediately followed by a pronoun. To make sure you use the correct pronoun, delete the noun from the pair. Look at the following examples to see how this is done.

They hired (we, us) **temporary workers.**

They hired **us.**

The management threw (we, us) **retirees** a small party.

The management threw **us** a small party.

INCOMPLETE CONSTRUCTIONS

Sometimes a pronoun comes at the end of a sentence following a comparative word such as *than* or *as*.

Maria spent more money than (they, them).

His young son is now taller than (I, me).

Bradley can wax floors better than (I, me).

The long walk tired us more than (they, them)

These sentences are called **incomplete constructions** because the complete meaning is only implied, not written out in its entirety. To figure out which pronoun is correct, complete the sentence in your head and use the pronoun that makes more sense.

Maria spent more money than *they did.*

His young son is now taller than *I am.*

Some sentences can be completed both ways. When this is true, choose the pronoun that makes more sense.

Bradley can play guitar better than *I can.*

Bradley can play guitar better than *he can play me.*

The first sentence makes more sense, so *I* is the correct pronoun.

The long walk tired us more than *they did.*

The long walk tired us more than *it did them.*

The second sentence makes more sense, so *them* is the correct choice.

Pronoun choice is especially important if the sentence makes sense either way. The following sentence can be completed using both pronouns, either of which makes good sense. The pronoun choice controls the meaning. Choose the pronoun that conveys the intended meaning.

I work with Assad more than (she, her).

I work with Assad more than *she does.*

I work with Assad more than *I work with her.*

AMBIGUOUS PRONOUN REFERENCES

Sometimes a sentence is written in such a way that a pronoun can refer to more than one antecedent. When this happens, we say the meaning is ambiguous; that is, it can be understood in more than one way. In the following examples, the ambiguous pronouns are italicized, and the possible antecedents are underlined.

As <u>Claude</u> spoke to the his girlfriend's <u>father</u>, *he* was very nervous.

Take the <u>door</u> from the <u>frame</u> and paint *it.*

<u>Theresa</u> told <u>Julia</u> *she* should get ready to go.

See how the sentences are rewritten below to clarify the ambiguous references.

> Claude was very nervous when he spoke to his girlfriend's father.
>
> Paint the door after taking it off the frame.
>
> Theresa told Julia to get ready to go.

REFLEXIVE PRONOUNS

Reflexive pronouns refer to the self as an object. They are called reflexive because they reflect the self like a mirror. Reflexive pronouns include the word *self* or *selves: myself, yourself, himself, herself, ourselves, themselves*. These pronouns reflect: *my* to *self, your* to *self*, and so on. The following sentences show how these pronouns are used in writing.

> Karen appointed *herself* to the committee.
>
> I booked the flight *myself*.
>
> Help *yourself* to more dessert.
>
> The neighbors keep to *themselves*.

USING REFLEXIVE PRONOUNS CORRECTLY

- The possessive pronouns *his* and *their* cannot be made reflexive.

    Wrong: The Garrets decided to supervise the building theirselves.

    Correct: The Garrets decided to supervise the building themselves.

    Wrong: Mitchell asked to do the work hisself.

    Correct: Mitchell asked to do the work himself.

- Avoid using a reflexive pronoun when a personal pronoun works in the sentence.

    Wrong: A group of volunteers and myself repaired the roof.

    Correct: A group of volunteers and I repaired the roof.

    Wrong: The results of the election were known only to myself.

    Correct: The results of the election were known only to me.

    Wrong: The responsibility is split between Jamison and yourself.

    Correct: The responsibility is split between Jamison and you.

Practice

Choose the correct pronoun in each of the following sentences. Check your work with the answers at the end of the chapter.

17. (We, Us) patients are pleased with our care.
18. The risk of this operation scared the doctor more than (we, us).
19. Penny and (I, me, myself) are planning a summer trip.
20. My brother drives much faster than (I, me).

Answers

1. her
2. his
3. his
4. he
5. himself
6. it
7. her
8. his
9. them
10. his, he
11. he, me
12. he
13. I
14. him, me
15. her, them
16. I
17. We
18. (it scared) us
19. I
20. I (do)

CHAPTER | 17

Do *you're* and *your* confuse you? How about *lie* and *lay,* or *sit* and *set*? Knowing how to use problem words correctly makes you a better writer.

PROBLEM VERBS AND PRONOUNS

This chapter covers problem verbs such as *lie/lay, sit/set, rise/raise,* and their various forms. It also covers problem pronouns such as *its/it's, your/you're, whose/who's, who/that/which,* and *there/they're/their.* You can distinguish yourself as a competent writer if you know how to use these properly.

PROBLEM VERBS
LIE/LAY

Few people use *lie* and *lay* correctly, perhaps because few people know the difference in meaning between the two. The verb *lie* means "to rest or recline." The verb *lay* means "to put or place." *Lie* is something you do yourself (or some person does himself or herself, or some object does itself); *lay* is something you do to an object. The table below shows the principal parts of each of these verbs. Their meanings, written in the correct form, appear in parentheses.

Present	Progressive (used with *am, is, are*)	Past	Past Participle (used with *have, has,* or *had*)
lie, lies (rest, rests)	lying (resting)	lay (rested)	lain (rested)
lay, lays (place, places)	laying (placing)	laid (placed)	laid (placed)

To choose the correct form of *lie* or *lay*, simply look at the meanings in parentheses. Choose the word in parentheses that makes the most sense and use the corresponding form of *lie* or *lay*. Sometimes none of the words seem right. In that case, choose the option that makes more sense than any of the others. If a sentence contains the word *down*, mentally delete the word from the sentence to make the appropriate verb more obvious. These sample sentences show how this is done.

The frisbee is _____ in the middle of the lawn. (Requires progressive)

Resting makes better sense than *placing*.

Choose *lying*.

Della asked Lisa to _____ the newspaper on the kitchen table. (Requires present)

Place makes better sense than *rest*.

Choose *lay*.

Yesterday, the snake _____ all day in the sun next to our house. (Requires past.)

Rested makes better sense than *placed*.

Choose *lay*.

Yesterday afternoon, I _____ down for a nap. (Requires past)

Remove the word *down*.

Rested makes better sense than *placed*.

Choose *lay*.

Sonja remembered that she had _____ the books on her desk. (Requires past participle)

> *Placed* makes better sense than *rested*.
>
> Choose *laid*.

Practice

Write the correct form of *lie* or *lay* in each of the blanks below. Check your work with the answers at the end of the chapter.

1. Huey _____ in bed for another hour after the alarm went off.

2. _____ the papers next to the copy machine.

3. The mail _____ on the dining room table.

4. The student _____ his assignment on the teacher's desk.

5. Who knew how long the confidential documents had _____ in the open or who had _____ them there in the first place?

SIT/SET

These two verbs are very similar to *lie* and *lay*. *Sit* means "to rest." *Set* means "to put or place." The table below shows the principal parts of each of these verbs. Their meanings, written in the correct form, appear in parentheses.

Present	Progressive (used with *am, is, are*)	Past	Past Participle (used with *have, has,* or *had*)
sit, sits (rest, rests)	sitting (resting)	sat (rested)	sat (rested)
set, sets (put, place; puts, places)	setting (putting, placing)	set (put, placed)	set (placed)

Choose the correct form of *sit* or *set* by using the meanings (the words in parentheses) in the sentence first. Decide which meaning makes the most sense, then choose the corresponding form of *sit* or *set*. See how this is done in the example sentences below.

> The actor _____ the props off in the wings.
>
> *Put* or *placed* makes more sense than *rested*.
>
> Choose *set*.

The judge _____ in the chair next to the bailiff.

Rested makes more sense than *put* or *placed*.

Choose *sat*.

Practice

Write the correct form of *sit* or *set* in each of the blanks below.

6. Our family _____ aside money for vacation.

7. Carol's car is the one _____ closest to the entrance.

8. Adam remembered where he _____ the packages down.

9. Scott _____ down behind to me and _____ his briefcase on the floor.

10. The parents had _____ in the waiting room for most of the morning.

RISE/RAISE

The verb *rise* means "to go up." The verb *raise* means "to move something up." *Raise* requires an object. In other words, something must receive the action of the verb *raise* (raise your hand, raise the flag, raise the objection, raise children). The table below shows the principal parts of both verbs.

Present	Progressive (used with *am, is, are*)	Past	Past Participle (used with *have, has,* or *had*)
rises, rise (goes up, go up) (comes up, come up)	rising (going up) (coming up)	rose (went up) (came up)	risen (gone up) (come up)
raises, raise (moves up, move up)	raising (moving up)	raised (moving up)	raised (moving up)

Choose the correct form of *rise* or *raise* by using the meanings (the words in parentheses) in the sentence first. Decide which meaning makes the most sense, then choose the corresponding form of *rise* or *raise*. See how this is done in the example sentences below. Sometimes none of the words seem especially appropriate. In that case, choose the option that makes more sense than any of the others.

The moon _____ a little bit later each evening.
> *Comes up* makes the most sense.
> Choose *rises*.

The crowd began to _____ their voices.
> *Move up* makes the most sense.
> Choose *raise*.

The water level _____ over a foot in the last day.
> *Went up* makes the most sense.
> Choose *rose*.

Practice

Write the correct form of *rise* or *raise* in each of the blanks below.

11. The custodian _____ the flag every morning before the sun _____.
12. The farmer _____ corn and soybeans.
13. The fog had _____ enough for us to see beyond the next hill.
14. The church members _____ from the pews to _____ a prayer.

PROBLEM PRONOUNS
Its/It's

Its is a possessive pronoun that means "belonging to it." *It's* is a contraction for *it is* or *it has*. The only time you will ever use *it's* is when you can also substitute the words *it is* or *it has*. Take time to make this substitution, and you will never confuse these two words.

> The thermometer in the roast will measure *its* (belonging to the roast) temperature.
> *It's* (it is) time for us to say goodbye and head home.
> *It's* (it has) been three years now since I've seen Tom.

Practice

Choose the correct word in each set of parentheses below. Check your work with the answers at the end of the chapter.

15. I wonder if (its, it's) a good idea for us to be here.
16. The wind will eventually stop (its, it's) howling.

17. Tell me when (its, it's) time for a break.

18. (Its, It's) been fun to watch the dog chase (its, it's) tail.

YOUR/YOU'RE

Your is a possessive pronoun that means "belonging to you." *You're* is a contraction for the words *you are.* The only time you should ever use *you're* is when you can also substitute the words *you are.* Take time to make this substitution, and you will never confuse these two words.

Is this *your* (belonging to you) new assignment?

When *you're* (you are) done, I want to talk to you.

Your (belonging to you) mother called this morning.

You're (you are) the recipient of this year's award.

Practice

Choose the correct word in each set of parentheses below. Check your work with the answers at the end of the chapter.

19. (Its, It's) (your, you're) turn to do the dishes.

20. Bring (your, you're) fishing pole along if (your, you're) coming.

21. (Your, You're) scheduled to work late this evening.

22. (Your, You're) plan seems to have worked.

WHO/THAT/WHICH

Who refers to people. *That* refers to things. *Which* is generally used to introduce nonessential clauses that describe things. (See Chapter 6 to review nonessential clauses.) Look at the following sentences to see how each of these words is used.

- **Who** refers to people.

    There is the woman *who* designed this building.

    The man *who* fixes my car has retired.

- **That** refers to things.

    This is the neighborhood *that* I told you about.

    The print *that* I wanted has been sold.

- **Which** introduces nonessential clauses—unless they refer to people, in which case you use *who.*

> Douglas, *who* plays in a local band, lives upstairs.
> My son, *who* loves to play video games, turns sixteen tomorrow.
> Vickie picked up a copy of *People, which* is her favorite magazine.
> The Mississippi River, *which* originates in Minnesota, empties into the Gulf of Mexico.

Practice

Choose the correct word in each set of parentheses below. Check your work with the answers at the end of the chapter.

23. Uncle Tim is the one (who, which, that) arranged this meeting.
24. This is the coat (who, which, that) I bought last year.
25. Rod Stewart, (who, which, that) is my favorite singer, has never won a Grammy award.
26. Interstate 235, (who, which, that) runs through town, is being repaired this summer.
27. There's the young man (who, which, that) wishes to speak with you.

WHOSE/WHO'S

Whose is a possessive pronoun that means "belonging to whom." *Who's* is a contraction for the words *who is* or *who has.* Take time to make this substitution, and you will never confuse these two words.

> *Who's* (Who is) handling the funeral arrangements?
> *Whose* (belonging to whom) bright idea was that?
> This is the officer *who's* (who is) on duty tonight.
> That is the girl *whose* (belonging to whom) picture was in the paper.

THERE/THEIR/THEY'RE

There is an adverb telling where an action or item is located. *Their* is a possessive pronoun that shows ownership. *They're* is a contraction for the words *they are.* Of all the confused word groups, this one is misused most often. Here is an easy way to distinguish among these words.

- Take a close look at this version of the word *tHERE.* You can see that it contains the word *here.* Wherever you use the word *there,* you should be able to substitute the word *here,* and the sentence should still make sense.

There (here) goes my future.

The supplies are in *there* (here).

- *Their* means "belonging to them." If you can insert this phrase after *their* in a sentence and the meaning remains the same, *their* is correct.

    Their (belonging to them) time is limited.

    This is *their* (belonging to them) problem, not mine.

- Finally, imagine that the apostrophe in *they're* is actually a very small letter *a.* If you change *they're* to *they are* in a sentence, you'll never misuse the word. Look over the example sentences below.

    They're (they are) hoping to leave in the morning.

    Do you know how *they're* (they are) going to arrange the schedule?

Practice

Choose the correct word in each set of parentheses below. Check your work with the answers at the end of the chapter.

28. (Your, You're) likely to lose your mind in (there, their, they're).
29. (There, Their, They're) rearranging the shelves in the closet.
30. (Its, It's) been a year since (there, their, they're) last anniversary.
31. The landscaper (who, which, that) did the work lives over (there, their, they're).
32. (Who's, Whose) been calling you all evening?
33. (Who's, Whose) idea was it take this shortcut?
34. Martha asked for the one (who's, whose) in charge of accounting.
35. (Who's, Whose) retirement are we celebrating?

Answers

1. lay	**12.** raised or raises	**24.** that
2. Lay	**13.** risen	**25.** who
3. lay	**14.** rose, raise	**26.** which
4. laid	**15.** it's	**27.** who
5. lain, laid	**16.** its	**28.** You're, there
6. set	**17.** it's	**29.** They're
7. sitting	**18.** It's, its	**30.** It's, their
8. set	**19.** It's, your	**31.** who, there
9. sat, set	**20.** your, you're	**32.** Who's
10. sat	**21.** You're	**33.** Whose
11. raised, rose or raises, rises	**22.** Your	**34.** who's
	23. who	**35.** Whose

Adjectives and adverbs can brighten writing and make it more specific and interesting—so that it communicates your ideas more fully. This chapter explains how to use modifiers correctly.

DRESSING WORDS FOR SUCCESS WITH MODIFIERS

Words that describe other words are called *modifiers*. *Adjectives* modify, or describe, nouns and pronouns. *Adverbs* modify, or describe, verbs, adjectives, and other adverbs. Sometimes a group of words functions as a modifier. Modifiers play a vital part in communication. Using them correctly is an important skill.

ADJECTIVES

Adjectives describe a noun or pronoun in a sentence. Here is an easy way to tell if a word is an adjective. Adjectives answer one of three questions about another word in the sentence: *which one? what kind?* and *how many?* The table below illustrates this. The adjectives are italicized to make them easy to identify.

Which One?	What Kind?	How Many?
that cabinet	*willow* tree	*many* hints
the other tape	*orange* vest	*five* entrances
his first clue	*greedy* partner	*several* reasons

ADJECTIVES THAT FOLLOW VERBS

Pay special attention to adjectives that follow verbs. Sometimes the adjective follows a verb, but it describes a noun or pronoun that comes before the verb. The following sentences illustrate this. The italicized adjectives describe the underlined nouns.

>These <u>strawberries</u> taste *sour.* (sour strawberries)

>Rhonda's <u>change</u> of heart seemed *strange.* (strange change)

>The <u>pickles</u> are *salty.* (salty pickles)

FEWER/LESS, NUMBER/AMOUNT

Use the adjective *fewer* to modify plural nouns, or things that can be counted. Use *less* for singular nouns that represent a quantity or a degree. Most nouns to which an *s* can be added require the adjective *fewer.*

>Our new neighborhood has *fewer* children (plural noun) than our old one had.

>Denise has *less* time (singular noun) to spare than you do.

The same principle applies to the nouns *number* and *amount.* Use the noun *number* when referring to plural nouns, or things that can be counted. Use the noun *amount* when referring to nouns that are singular.

>The *number* of hours (plural noun) we estimated for this job was incorrect.

>The *amount* of time (singular noun) for our work was underestimated.

Practice

Choose the correct word in parentheses in each of the following sentences. Check your work with the answers at the end of the chapter.

1. The lawn has (fewer, less) weeds than it had last summer.
2. This side trip increased the (amount, number) of miles significantly.

3. This cutlery set costs (fewer, less) money than that one.

4. The (amount, number) of work involved does not justify the (amount, number) of people assigned to the job.

5. Phoebe remembers (fewer, less) about the old days than Grandpa does, but Grandpa tells (fewer, less) stories than Phoebe.

ADVERBS

Use adverbs to describe verbs, adjectives, and other adverbs. Here is an easy way to tell if a word is an adverb. Adverbs answer one of these questions about another word in the sentence: *where? when? how?* and *to what extent?* The adverbs are italicized in the table below.

Where?	When?	How?	To What Extent?
The car drove *forward.*	Marvin left *earlier.*	She yelled *loudly.*	Royce could *hardly* wait.
Put your baggage *below.*	Hank called *later.*	Turtles move *slowly.*	Dean *narrowly* missed an accident.
Look *here.*	We'll go *tomorrow.*	The loon called *mournfully.*	Marsha *still* doesn't understand.

The table below shows examples of adverbs modifying verbs, adjectives, and other adverbs. The adverbs are italicized.

Adverbs Modifying Verbs	Adverbs Modifying Adjectives	Adverbs Modifying Other Adverbs
Packages are mailed *regularly.*	an *extremely* annoying sound	*most clearly* explained
Children play *happily.*	a *strangely* quiet room	*quite reasonably* stated
Rescuers came *immediately.*	an *unusually* clean uniform	improve *rather slowly*

ADJECTIVE OR ADVERB?

Sometimes writers mistakenly use adjectives in place of adverbs. This is illustrated in the sentences on the next page. The italicized words are adjectives incorrectly used in place of adverbs. The adverb form follows the sentence.

Louise reads very *thorough*. (**thoroughly**)
Pack these dishes very *careful*. (**carefully**)
Vern sang as *loud* as he was able. (**loudly**)

Take special care to choose the correct word when using verbs that deal with the senses: *touch, taste, look, smell, sound*. If the word following the verb describes a noun or pronoun that comes before the verb, use an adjective. If the word following the verb describes the verb, use an adverb.

In each of the sets of examples below, the same verb is used. In one sentence, however, the word following the verb is an adjective. In the other sentence, the word following is an adverb. The parentheses explain how the word is used. Read the examples and take note of the differences.

The trainer felt gently around the player's ankle. (*Gently* is an adverb describing *felt*.)

The entire group felt sick after lunch. (*Sick* is an adjective describing *group*.)

The new sofa looked odd to me. (*Odd* is an adjective describing *sofa*.)

The judge looked skeptically at the attorney. (*Skeptically* is an adverb describing *looked*.)

The milk smelled sour to us. (*Sour* is an adjective describing *milk*.)

The doe smelled the feed hesitantly. (*Hesitantly* is used as an adverb describing *smelled*.)

Practice

Choose the correct word in parentheses in each of the following sentences. Check your work with the answers at the end of the chapter.

6. Anita sang the melody line (correct, correctly).
7. Patricia looked (tired, tiredly) after the long day.
8. This door doesn't shut as (easy, easily) as it used to.
9. These new boots feel more (comfortable, comfortably) than my old ones.
10. Ask (polite, politely) if you need help with your work.
11. The doctor walked (slow, slowly) out of the operating room.
12. Jay seems (unhappy, unhappily) about the test results.
13. The woman looked (angry, angrily) as she left the hair salon.

14. The burglar felt (careful, carefully) for the alarm switch.

15. The steam treatment cleaned our carpets (thorough, thoroughly).

GOOD AND WELL, BAD AND BADLY

Good and *bad* are adjectives. *Well* and *badly* are adverbs. Sometimes *good* and *bad* are mistakenly used to describe a verb. Use *well* and *badly* to describe an action.

> Elizabeth performed *well* (or *badly)* at her recital. (*Well* or *badly* describes *performed,* a verb.)
>
> Carolyn felt *good* (or *bad*) after her treatment. (*Good* or *bad* describes *Carolyn,* a noun.)
>
> The condominiums were *well* (or *badly*) built. (*Well* or *badly* describes *built,* a verb.)
>
> The coffee smelled *good* (or *bad)* when I walked into the house. (*Good* or *bad* describes *coffee,* a noun.)

Practice

Choose the correct word in parentheses in each of the following sentences. Check your work with the answers at the end of the chapter.

16. Pasta does not taste as (good, well) if it is overcooked.

17. Paulina felt (bad, badly) after the workout.

18. Janelle did (good, well) on her annual performance review.

19. This new arrangement works very (good, well).

20. The touring choir sang quite (bad, badly).

COMPARISONS

Adjectives and adverbs change form when they are used in comparisons. When you compare two things, use the comparative form of the modifier. If you are comparing more than two things, use the superlative form of the modifier.

CREATING THE COMPARATIVE FORM

To compare two things, you can either:

- add *er* to the modifier, or
- place the word *more* or *less* before the modifier

Add *er* to short modifiers (one or two syllables). Use *more* and *less* with modifiers of more than two syllables.

CREATING THE SUPERLATIVE FORM

To compare more than two things, you can either:
- add *est* to the modifier, or
- place the word *most* or *least* before the modifier

BETWEEN /AMONG

When comparing items in a prepositional phrase, use *between* for two items, *among* for three or more.

Look at the samples in the table below. Some modifiers change form completely. The first six lines of the table illustrate these special modifiers.

Modifier	Comparative (for two items)	Superlative (more than two)
good	better	best
well	better	best
many	more	most
much	more	most
bad	worse	worst
little	less or lesser	least
neat	neater	neatest
lovely	lovelier	loveliest
funny	funnier	funniest
extreme	more [or less] extreme	most [or least] extreme
intelligent	more [or less] intelligent	most [or least] intelligent
precisely	more [or less] precisely	most [or least] precisely
	between	among

See how the comparative and superlative forms are used in the following sentences.

Down is a *better* direction for my weight to be going. (comparing two directions)

This stereo sounds *better* than any of the others. (comparing two stereos many times)

The original minerals were *more thoroughly* filtered than those you buy today. (compares two minerals)

Leech Lake is the *best* walleye lake around. (comparing more than two lakes)

These results show the *greatest* improvement so far. (comparing more than two sets of results)

Practice

Choose the correct word in parentheses in each of the following sentences. Check your work with the answers at the end of the chapter.

21. The Ford Taurus is the (large, larger, largest) selling mid-size car.
22. Heavy cover is the (more, most) promising habitat for pheasants.
23. Charlotte is the (younger, youngest) of the twins and the (shorter, shortest) one in the entire family.
24. Divide my land (among, between) my two sons, but split the money (among, between) all of my children.
25. The decorator chose the (more, most) unusual color scheme I've ever seen.

AVOIDING ILLOGICAL OR UNCLEAR COMPARISONS

"Cassidy is braver than any Western hero," is an illogical statement. It implies that Cassidy, who is a Western hero, is braver than himself. Always include the words *other* or *else* to keep your comparisons from being illogical.

Cassidy is braver than any **other** Western hero.

Sid can track better than anyone **else** in the group.

AVOIDING DOUBLE COMPARISONS

A double comparison occurs when a writer uses both *er* or *est* and *more/less* or *most/least*.

Wrong	Correct
Horace is the most rudest man I know.	Horace is the rudest man I know.
These instructions are more clearer.	These instructions are clearer.
Ethel is more pickier about her kitchen than I am.	Ethel is pickier about her kitchen than I am.

AVOIDING DOUBLE NEGATIVES

When a negative word such as *not* or *no* is added to a statement that is already negative, a double negative results. Avoid double negatives in your writing. The words *hardly* and *barely* are also negative words. In the example sentences below, the negative words are highlighted. Pay close attention to how the incorrect sentences are rewritten to avoid the double negative.

Wrong	Correct
The store **doesn't** have **no** nails that size.	The store **doesn't** have any nails that size. The store has **no** nails that size.
We **don't** want **no** dessert.	We **don't** want any dessert. We want **no** dessert.
I **don't barely** have money for a soda.	I **don't** have money for a soda. I **barely** have money for a soda.
I **can't hardly** hear you.	I can **hardly** hear you. I **can't** hear you.

MISPLACED MODIFIERS

Place words, phrases, or clauses that describe nouns and pronouns as closely as possible to the words they describe. Failure to do this often results in a **misplaced modifier** and a sentence that means something other than what was intended.

PLACEMENT OF WORDS THAT MODIFY

The words *only, almost,* and *just* should be placed as close as possible to the word described. The best place is right before the words they describe. The placement of the word, phrase, or clause affects the meaning of the sentence.

> The woman **only** looked at two chairs.
> The woman looked at **only** two chairs.

The first sentence above implies that the woman "only looked" at the chairs, but nothing else; she didn't sit in them or touch them. The second sentence above explains that she looked at "only two" samples, not three or four. The placement of the word *only* changes the meaning of the sentence.

Look at another pair of sentences:

Josh **nearly** scored four touchdowns.

Josh scored **nearly** four touchdowns.

In the first sentence above, Josh "nearly scored," or came very close to the goal line four times without actually crossing. In the second sentence above, Josh scored "nearly four" touchdowns—maybe 3 1/2. How many points are awarded for that?

Here's an example using *just:*

The delivery company **just** rents its vans.

The delivery company rents **just** its vans.

In the first sentence above, the company "just rents" its vans, rather than buying them. The second sentence above suggests that the company rents "just its vans," not any of its other vehicles, perhaps cars or trucks.

PLACEMENT OF PHRASES AND CLAUSES THAT MODIFY

Phrases and clauses that describe nouns or pronouns must also be placed as closely as possible to the words they describe. The sentences in the table below contain misplaced modifiers. Pay close attention to how they are rewritten to clarify the meaning.

Sentences with Misplaced Modifiers	Corrected Versions
My uncle told me about feeding cattle in the kitchen. (What are cattle doing in the kitchen?)	In the kitchen, my uncle told me about feeding cattle. My uncle told me about feeding cattle while we were in the kitchen.
A huge python followed the man that was slithering slowly through the grass. (Why was the man slithering through the grass?)	A huge python that was slithering slowly through the grass followed the man. Slithering slowly through the grass, a huge python followed the man.

DANGLING MODIFIERS

Words, phrases, or clauses that begin a sentence and are set off by commas sometimes mistakenly modify the wrong noun or pronoun.

These are called **dangling modifiers.** The sentences in the following table contain dangling modifiers. Pay close attention to how they are rewritten to avoid the problem.

Sentences with Dangling Modifiers	Corrected Versions
While talking on the telephone, the potatoes boiled over. (Why were the potatoes talking on the telephone?)	While I was talking on the telephone, the potatoes boiled over. The potatoes boiled over while I talked on the phone.
Nailed to a utility pole, Jason saw the sign. (Why was Jason nailed to a utility pole?)	Jason saw the sign nailed to a utility pole. Nailed to the utility pole, the sign was visible to Jason.
Broken and beyond repair, Grandma threw the serving dish away. (Why was Grandma broken?)	Grandma threw away the broken serving dish that was beyond repair. Broken and beyond repair, the serving dish was thrown away by Grandma.

Practice

Choose the correctly written sentence from each of the following sets.

26. a. Sylvan likes eggs fried in butter.

    b. Fried in butter, Sylvan likes eggs.

27. a. Janette likes fresh fish better than any meat.

    b. Janette likes fresh fish better than any other meat.

28. a. At the age of three, Grandpa took me fishing.

    b. When I was three, Grandpa took me fishing.

29. a. Dennis is quicker than anybody on the team. (Dennis is a team member.)

    b. Dennis is quicker than anybody else on the team.

30. a. I can't hardly understand why we're still waiting.

    b. I can't understand why we're still waiting.

31. a. Growling softly, a big dog approached the boy.

    b. A big dog approached the boy that was growling softly.

32. a. This floor doesn't need no more wax.

    b. This floor doesn't need any more wax.

33. a. The speaker would only answer two questions.

    b. The speaker would answer only two questions.

34. a. While barbecuing our steaks, a hungry salesman walked into the backyard.

    b. A hungry salesman walked into the backyard while we were barbecuing our steaks.

35. a. Swinging from branch to branch, I saw the spider monkey.

    b. I saw the spider monkey swinging from branch to branch.

Answers

1. fewer	**19.** well
2. number	**20.** badly
3. less	**21.** largest
4. amount, number	**22.** most
5. less, fewer	**23.** younger, shortest
6. correctly	**24.** between, among
7. tired	**25.** most
8. easily	**26.** a
9. comfortable	**27.** b
10. politely	**28.** b
11. slowly	**29.** b
12. unhappy	**30.** b
13. angry	**31.** a
14. carefully	**32.** b
15. thoroughly	**33.** b
16. good	**34.** b
17. bad	**35.** b
18. well	

CHAPTER | 19

Brake or break? Than or then? Accept or except? This chapter explains the meanings of easily confused words. If you keep track of the meanings, you can avoid misusing words in your writing. This chapter makes it easy.

TRICKY WORDS

This chapter covers some of the most commonly confused word pairs. If you learn to distinguish between these words, you can avoid errors in your writing. The words are divided into five separate sections, with practice exercises at the end of each section.

PART ONE
BRAKE/BREAK

- **Brake** as a verb means *slow* or *stop*. As a noun it means *hindrance, drag*.

- **Break** as a verb means *separate, shatter, adjourn.* As a noun it means *separation, crack, pause, opportunity.*

  During our *break* (pause) we asked the sergeant if we could *break* (separate) rank.

  Brake (slow) gently if you're on packed snow by applying slight pressure to the *brake* (drag).

  Dustin Hoffman's big *break* (opportunity) came when he took a role in *Midnight Cowboy.*

PASSED/PAST

- **Passed** is a verb, the past tense of *pass,* meaning *transferred, went ahead* or *by, elapsed, finished.*
- **Past** as a noun means *history.* As an adjective it means *former.*

  It's best not to dig up the *past* (history) in this family.

  An hour *passed* (elapsed) before the X-rays returned from the lab.

  Mae *passed* (finished) the test she took yesterday.

  Ken Griffey *passed* (transferred) his baseball talent to his son.

  I know I lived near water in a *past* (former) life.

  The race cars *passed* (went by) the stands at over 200 miles per hour.

PEACE/PIECE

- **Peace** is a noun meaning *tranquility.*
- **Piece** as a noun means *division, bit, creation.* As a verb it means *patch, repair.*

  We could have some *peace* (tranquility) around here if you would just *piece* (patch) together the few remaining *pieces* (bits) of your mind.

PLAIN/PLANE

- **Plain** is an adjective meaning *ordinary, clear, simple, flat country.*
- **Plane** is a noun meaning *airship, flat surface, level.*

  Nomadic tribes roamed the *plain* (flat country).

  Helen prefers *plain* (ordinary) vegetables.

  The answer is *plain* (clear) to me.

  The commune adopted a very *plain* (simple) lifestyle.

  The pilot flew the *plane* (airship) on a *plane* (level).

SCENE/SEEN

- **Scene** is a noun meaning *view, site, commotion.*
- **Seen** is a verb, the past participle of *see,* meaning *observed, noticed.*

> The crowd caused a *scene* (commotion) at the *scene* (site) of the fight, the most confused sight the rookie officer had ever *seen* (observed).

Practice

Choose the correct word in each of the following sentences. Check your work with the answers at the end of the chapter.

1. Cedric hit the (brake, break) as he noticed the truck ahead (brake, break) to avoid a (brake, break) in the road.
2. The rookie second baseman (passed, past) the record set in the (passed, past) year.
3. We hope this (peace, piece) of information will give you (peace, piece) of mind.
4. The (plain, plane) gasoline won't work to fuel this (plain, plane).
5. Scottie's parents hadn't (scene, seen) the most violent (scene, seen) in the show.

PART TWO
BY/BUY

- **By** is a preposition used to introduce a phrase: *by the book, by the time, by the way.*
- **Buy** as a verb means *purchase.* As a noun it means *bargain, deal.*

> Carter stopped *by* (preposition) the store to *buy* (purchase) some albums he thought were a great *buy* (deal).

DEAR/DEER

- **Dear** is an adjective meaning *valued, loved.*
- **Deer** is a noun referring to a four-legged animal that lives in the woods and looks like Bambi.

> The *dear* (loved) family was killed when their car struck a *deer* (four-legged animal).

DIE/DYE

- **Die** is a verb meaning *pass away, fade.*
- **Dye** as a verb means *color, tint.* As a noun, it means *coloring, pigment.*

> The speaker waited for the noise to *die* (fade).
>
> We plan to *dye* (color) the shirts orange.

WEAK/WEEK

- **Weak** is an adjective meaning *flimsy, frail, powerless.*
- **Week** is a noun meaning *seven days.*

> The signal from the lost plane was so *weak* (frail) that rescuers took a *week* (seven days) to locate it.

WHICH/WITCH

- **Which** is a pronoun. Use *which* in a sentence dealing with a choice: *Which* one do you want? Also, use *which* to introduce a nonessential clause: This car, *which* I have never driven, is the one I'm thinking about buying.
- **Witch** is a noun meaning *sorceress, enchantress.*

> Can you tell me *which* (choice word) *witch* (enchantress) to believe?

Practice

Choose the correct word in each of the following sentences. Check your work with the answers at the end of the chapter.

6. If the fax machine isn't repaired (by, buy) morning, we'll have to (by, buy) another one.
7. We waited to (die, dye) the sheets, hoping the wind would (die, dye) down.
8. This animal is too (weak, week) to survive for more than a (weak, week).
9. My (dear, deer) child, you'll never see a (dear, deer) if you watch the sky.
10. The (which, witch) couldn't decide (which, witch) cat to take on Halloween.

PART THREE
HEAR/HERE
- **Hear** is a verb meaning *listen to.*
- **Here** means *in this place, to this place.*

> Come *here* (to this place) so you can *hear* (listen to) this recording.

HOLE/WHOLE
- **Hole** is a noun meaning *opening, gap, dent.*
- **Whole** as an adjective means *entire, intact.* As a noun, it means *entire part* or *amount.*

> The *whole* (entire) pie was eaten.
> The attendant repaired the *hole* (opening) in the tire.

KNEW/NEW
- **Knew** is a verb, the past tense of *know,* meaning *understood, recognized.*
- **New** is an adjective meaning *fresh, different, current.*

> I *knew* (understood) he was looking for a *new* (different) approach.

KNOW/NO
- **Know** is a verb meaning *understand, recognize.*
- **No** means *not so, not any, not at all.* As an adjective it means *none, not one.*

> I *know* (understand), we have *no* (not any) more money in this account.

MEAT/MEET
- **Meat** is a noun meaning *food, flesh, main part.*
- **Meet** as a verb means *assemble, greet, fulfill.* As a noun, it means *assembly.*

> The chefs will *meet* (assemble) to select the *meat* (flesh) for the dinner.

Practice
Choose the correct word in each of the following sentences. Check your work with the answers at the end of the chapter.

11. You'll (hear, here) better if you stand (hear, here).

12. This (hole, whole) means this (hole, whole) balloon is worthless.

13. Hans was the only one who (knew, new) how to operate the (knew, new) press.

14. I (know, no) we expect (know, no) further trouble from you.

15. The hunters will (meat, meet) at the locker plant to split up the (meat, meet) from the deer.

PART FOUR
ADVICE/ADVISE

- **Advice,** a noun meaning *suggestion* or *suggestions,* rhymes with *ice* and also includes that word: *advICE.*
- **Advise** is a verb meaning *suggest to, warn.*

> We *advise* (warn) you to heed the *advice* (suggestions) of your attorney.

AFFECT/EFFECT

- **Affect** as a verb means *alter, inspire, move emotionally, imitate.* As an adjective, it means *imitated, pretended.*
- **Effect** as a noun means *consequence* or *result.* As a verb, it means *cause.*

> King's moving "I Have a Dream" speech will *affect* (inspire) listeners for many generations.
>
> How will this *affect* (alter) the outcome?
>
> Merle's *affected* (pretended) accent annoyed his friends.
>
> What *effect* (consequence) does cold weather have on tropical plants?
>
> Will it *effect* (cause) a change?

ONE/WON

- **One** is an adjective meaning *single.* It can also be used as pronoun to replace a person, place, or thing.
- **Won** is verb meaning *prevailed, achieved, acquired.*

> Lynette is the *one* (referring to Lynette) who *won* (acquired) over *one* (single) million dollars in the lottery.

SEAM/SEEM

- **Seam** is a noun meaning *joint, joining point.*
- **Seem** is a verb meaning *appear.*

> It *seems* (appears) to me that this *seam* (joining point) is coming apart.

WEATHER/WHETHER

- **Weather** is a noun referring to the condition outside.
- **Whether** means *if* and is used when referring to a possibility or choice.

> We won't know *whether* (if) we'll come until we know what the *weather* (condition outside) is going to do.

Practice

Choose the correct word in each of the following sentences. Check your work with the answers at the end of the chapter.

16. The psychic will (advice, advise) you to seek (advice, advise) often.
17. We won't know the (affect, effect) of this change on production until we know how it will (affect, effect) worker morale.
18. If I (one, won) the match, I would be the only (one, won) to have (one, won) more than (one, won) championship ring.
19. Does this (seam, seem) (seam, seem) loose to you?
20. Do you know (weather, whether) this awful (weather, whether) will continue into tomorrow?

PART FIVE
CHOOSE/CHOSE

- **Choose** is a verb meaning *select.* It rhymes with *bruise.*
- **Chose** is also a verb, the past tense of *choose,* meaning *selected.* It rhymes with *hose.*

> The neighbors *chose* (selected) not to participate in the neighborhood party.
>
> Next time, they should *choose* (select) more wisely.

LOOSE/LOSE/LOSS

- **Loose** is an adjective meaning *free, unrestrained, not tight.* It rhymes with *goose.*

- **Lose** is a verb meaning to *misplace,* to *be defeated, fail to keep.* It rhymes with *shoes.*
- **Loss** is a noun meaning the *opposite of victory or gain, defeat, downturn.* It rhymes with *toss.*

> The cattle ran *loose* (free) in the pasture.
>
> The knot in this shoelaces is *loose* (not tight).
>
> If you *lose* (misplace) your place in line, it means a serious *loss* (opposite of gain) of time.

THAN/THEN

- **Than** is a conjunctive word used to make a comparison.
- **Then** means *next* or tells when.

> First we'll eat; *then* (next) we'll discuss ways to make this season more successful *than* (comparison) our last one.

SUPPOSE/SUPPOSED

- **Suppose** is a verb meaning *assume, imagine.*
- **Supposed** as a verb, the past tense of *suppose,* means *assumed, imagined.* As an adjective, it means *expected, obligated.*

> I *suppose* (assume) we can finish this load.
>
> The bricklayers *supposed* (assumed) the foundation would be ready.
>
> The concrete was *supposed* (expected) to have cured by morning.

USE/USED

- **Use** as a verb means *utilize, deplete.* As a noun, it means *purpose.*
- **Used** as a verb is the past tense of *use,* meaning *utilized, depleted.* As an adjective, it means *secondhand.*
- **Used to** means *accustomed to* or *formerly.*

> You can *use* (utilize) the same process you *used* (utilized) yesterday.
>
> What is the *use* (purpose) of buying *used* (secondhand) equipment if it doesn't work?
>
> We *used to* (formerly) talk regularly before we became *used to* (accustomed to) long periods of silence.

Practice

Choose the correct word in each of the following sentences. Check your work with the answers at the end of the chapter.

21. (Choose, Chose) your words carefully.
22. Nigel (choose, chose) not to participate in the games.
23. A (loose, lose, loss) today means we'll (loose, lose, loss) our first place spot.
24. The turkeys ran (loose, lose, loss) in the yard.
25. The joint should remain (loose, lose, loss) so you won't (loose, lose, loss) flexibility.
26. Don't (loose, lose, loss) your gloves.
27. Luann was (suppose, supposed) to come earlier today (than, then) yesterday.
28. We (use, used) to look at (use, used) cars, but now we've become (use, used) to driving new vehicles.
29. (Choose, Chose) your weapon; (than, then) stand back to back, step ten paces, turn, and fire.
30. Spending a quiet evening is more appealing (than, then) it (use, used) to be.

Answers

1. brake, brake, break
2. passed, past
3. piece, peace
4. plain, plane
5. seen, scene
6. by, buy
7. dye, die
8. weak, week
9. dear, deer
10. witch, which
11. hear, here
12. hole, whole
13. knew, new
14. know, no
15. meet, meat
16. advise, advice
17. effect, affect
18. won, one, won, one
19. seam, seem
20. whether, weather
21. Choose
22. chose
23. loss, lose
24. loose
25. loose, lose
26. lose
27. supposed, than
28. used, used, used
29. Choose, then
30. than, used

CHAPTER | 20

This chapter covers more confusing words: those that have three easily confused meanings, and those that are sometimes written as one word and sometimes as two. By the end of this chapter you'll know which ones to use and why.

MORE TRICKY WORDS

Here are some more of the most com— monly confused words that you are likely to use in your writing. If you learn to distinguish these words, you can avoid errors. The words are divided into three separate sections, with practice exercises at the end of each section.

THREE-WAY CONFUSION
To/Too/Two

- *To* is a preposition or part of an infinitive (used with a verb).

  Preposition: Use *to* for introducing a prepositional phrase that tells *where*: to the store, to the top, to my home, to our garden, to his laboratory, to his castle, to our advantage, to an open door, to a song, to the science room, etc.

Part of an infinitive: Use *to* as part of an infinitive (*to* followed by a verb, sometimes separated by an adverb): to run, to jump, to want badly, to seek, to propose, to write, to explode, to sorely need, to badly botch, to carefully examine, and so on.

- *Too* is an adverb meaning *also* or *very*. Wherever you use the word *too,* you should be able to substitute the word *also* or *very*.

- *Two* is an adjective, the name of a number, as in *one, two*.
    The couple went *to* (introduces a prepositional phrase) the deli *to* (introduces an infinitive phrase) pick up *two* (one, two) plate dinners because both of them were *too* (very) tired *to* (introduces an infinitive phrase) cook dinner.

THERE/THEIR/THEY'RE

- *There* is an adverb that refers to a the location of something or someone. Whenever you use the word *there,* you should also be able to substitute the word *here*.
- *Their* means "belonging to them." Use it as an adjective to show possession.
- *They're* is a short form, or contraction, of the words *they are*. Use *they're* only when you could also use the words *they are*.
    They're (they are) going *there* (a location) to see *their* (belonging to them) doctor.
    If *their* (belonging to them) children are in *there* (a location), *they're* (they are) in trouble.

LEAD/LED/LEAD

- *Lead* as a verb means to *guide* or *direct*. As a noun, it means *front position*. It rhymes with *seed*.
- *Led* is a verb, the past tense of *lead*, meaning *guided* or *directed*. It rhymes with *red*.

- *Lead* is also a noun, the name of a metal. It, too, rhymes with *red*.

  The Pied Piper took the *lead* (front position) and *led* (guided) the children out of Hamlin.

  The presence of *lead* (a metal) in the paint *led* (directed) us to think the house was old.

QUITE/QUIT/QUIET

- *Quite* is an adverb meaning *completely, very,* or *entirely*. It rhymes with *fight*.
- *Quit* is a verb meaning *stop, cease* or *stopped, ceased*. It rhymes with *sit*.
- *Quiet* as an adjective means *calm, silent, noiseless*. As a verb, it means to *soothe* or *calm*. As a noun, it means *tranquillity* or *peacefulness*. It rhymes with *riot*.

  Mother was *quite* (very) shocked when the children *quit* (stopped) playing and spent some *quiet* (calm) time in their rooms.

WHERE/WEAR/WERE

- *Where* is an adverb referring to a place or location.
- *Wear* as a verb means to *put on, tire,* or *deteriorate*. As a noun, it means *deterioration*.
- *Were* is a verb, the plural past tense of *be*.

  Where (a place) are the parts that showed excessive *wear* (deterioration)?

  You will *wear* (deteriorate) out this coat if you *wear* (put on) it all the time.

  Where (location) are the clothes you *were* planning to *wear* (put on) tomorrow?

Practice

Choose the correct form of the word in parentheses. Check your work with the answers at the end of the chapter.

1. Along with the lettuce, please get (to, too, two) avocados (to, too, two) when you go (to, too, two) the store.
2. They should put (there, their, they're) luggage in (there, their, they're).

3. If (there, their, they're) interested in improving (there, their, they're) health, I'll help them get (there, their, they're).

4. Two hours is (quiet, quit, quite) a long time for children to be (quiet, quit, quite).

5. The furnace (quiet, quit, quite) during the night, and it's (quiet, quit, quite) cold in the house.

6. Do you know (wear, were, where) I could (wear, were, where) something like this?

7. The horses (wear, were, where) restless today.

8. Ronald couldn't remember (wear, were, where) the cards (wear, were, where).

9. The foreman (led, lead) the workers out of the (led, lead) mine.

10. Kevin mounted the (led, lead) horse and (led, lead) the wagons into the mountains.

MORE THREE-WAY CONFUSION
ACCEPT/EXCEPT/EXPECT

- *Accept* is a verb meaning *receive* or *bear*.
- *Except* is a preposition meaning *but, excluding*.
- *Expect* is a verb meaning *anticipate, demand, assume*.

> Customers *expect* (demand) nothing *except* (but) a fair deal, I *expect* (assume).
>
> We *expect* (anticipate) they will *accept* (receive) our apology.
>
> Lorraine will *accept* (bear) the responsibility for making housing arrangements.

RIGHT/WRITE/RITE

- *Right* is an adjective meaning *correct, proper,* or the *opposite of left*.
- *Write* is a verb meaning *record* or *inscribe*.
- *Rite* is a noun meaning *ceremony* or *ritual*.

> The court reporter will *write* (record) the exact words of the testimony.
>
> The shaman will be able to perform the *rite* (ceremony) in the *right* (proper) way.
>
> It seems *right* (proper) that we record the *right* (correct) answer on the *right* (opposite of left) side.

THOUGH/THROUGH/THREW

- *Though* as a conjunction means *even if*. As an adverb, it means *however*.
- *Through* means *from one side to the other*.
- *Threw* is the past tense of the verb *throw*. It means *tossed*.

> *Though* (even if) you may think it's a waste, you should *throw* (toss) away outdated medication.
>
> Bibek *threw* (tossed) the ball *through* (from one side to the other) the window.

SENT/CENT/SCENT

- *Sent* is a verb, the past tense of *send*, meaning *dispatched* or *transmitted*.
- *Cent* is a noun meaning *one penny*, a coin worth one-hundredth of a dollar.
- *Scent* is a noun meaning *odor* or *smell*.

> You can buy this *scent* (odor) capsule for just a *cent* (one penny).
>
> The guide *sent* (dispatched) a message as soon as the dogs picked up the *scent* (odor).

SIGHT/SITE/CITE

- *Sight* as a noun means the *ability to see*. As a verb, it means *see, spot*.
- *Site* is a noun meaning *location* or *position*.
- *Cite* is a verb meaning *quote* or *make reference to*.

> At ninety the old man's *sight* (ability to see) was sharp enough to *sight* (spot) even the smallest character flaw.
>
> This is the proposed *site* (location) for our school.
>
> *Cite* (make reference to) the source of the information in your paper.

Practice

Choose the correct form of the word in parentheses. Check your work with the answers at the end of the chapter.

11. Our letter can be (sent, cent, scent) if we will add another (sent, cent, scent) of postage.

12. Bernice smelled the (sent, cent, scent) of cabbage when she walked into the kitchen.

13. The customers were (right, write, rite) in assuming the company would (right, write, rite) them a letter explaining the policy change.

14. The senior priest presides over the (right, write, rite) of confirmation.

15. The manufacturers (accept, except, expect) that we will (accept, except, expect) a partial delivery or our order.

16. The doctor walked (though, through, threw) the waiting room even (though, through, threw) the receptionist (though, through, threw) a fit every time she did so.

17. The quarterback (though, through, threw) the ball right (though, through, threw) the hands of the receiver.

18. Beyond the next hill you should be able to (sight, site, cite) the (sight, site, cite) for the new city park.

19. Researchers hope that their statistics will be (sighted, sited, cited) accurately.

20. Everyone (accept, except, expect) John Henry will (accept, except, expect) our charity.

ONE WORD OR TWO?

The words in this section are very much alike but have different meanings, depending on whether they are one word or two words.

ALREADY/ALL READY

- *Already* means *as early as this, previously, by this time.*
- *All ready* means *completely ready, totally ready.*
    > The dockhands had unloaded the warehouse *already* (as early as this).

    > The harvesters have *already* (previously, by this time) finished that field.

    > Is this print order *all ready* (completely ready) to go?

ALTOGETHER/ALL TOGETHER

- *Altogether* means *entirely, completely.*
- *All together* means *simultaneously.*
    > His testimony was *altogether* (entirely) true.

    > The fans moaned *all together* (simultaneously).

Everyday/Every Day

- *Everyday* means *ordinary, usual.*
- *Every day* means *each day.*

> I wore my *everyday* (ordinary) clothes.
>
> Inspectors examine the machinery *every day* (each day).

Maybe/May Be

- *Maybe* means *perhaps.*
- *May be* means *might be.*

> *Maybe* (perhaps) we will finish a day earlier than we had planned.
>
> On the other hand, we *may be* (might be) later than we thought.

ALWAYS TWO WORDS

The words in this section are often incorrectly written as one word.

All Right

- *Alright* is substandard usage. Avoid using this form in formal writing.
- *All right* means *completely fine, entirely good.*

> Your work seems *all right* (completely fine) to me.

A Lot

- *Alot* is substandard usage. Avoid using this form in formal writing. *A lot* means *much.*
- *Allot* is a word meaning to *portion out.*

> The committee should *allot* (portion out) *a lot* of (much) time for questions.

Practice

Choose the correct form of the word in parentheses. Check your work with the answers at the end of the chapter.

21. You (where, wear, were) your (everyday, every day) shoes almost (everyday, every day).
22. (Maybe, may be) if we change our approach, it (maybe, may be) the thing that will help us get back on track.

23. If the whole section had been (already, all ready) we could have (already, all ready) started this order.
24. They should be (alright, all right) if they read the directions.
25. If we get the whole family (altogether, all together), we should have (altogether, all together) enough people power to finishing moving everything out of the house.
26. Chester thought it was (all right, alright) to (a lot, allot) a few tickets for family members.
27. Patrick has (a lot, allot) of spare change.
28. Keith has (all ready, already) picked up our mail, but (may be, maybe) we can catch him before he leaves the building.
29. Guy (may be, maybe) able to deliver this speech if he can get his notes (all together, altogether).
30. Margaret leaves at 3:30 (every day, everyday).

Answers

1. two, too, to
2. their, there
3. they're, their, there
4. quite, quiet
5. quit, quite
6. where, wear
7. were
8. where, were
9. led, lead
10. lead, led
11. sent, cent
12. scent
13. right, write
14. rite
15. expect, accept
16. through, though, threw
17. threw, through
18. sight, site
19. cited
20. except, accept
21. wear, everyday, every day
22. Maybe, may be
23. all ready, already
24. all right
25. all together, altogether
26. all right, allot
27. a lot
28. already, maybe
29. may be, all together
30. every day

CONCLUSION

You've done it! You've made it through these lessons. If you have trouble with verbs in English, you should check out Appendix A, "Two-Word Verbs," which tells you how to use certain idiomatic verb forms. If you had fun or want to learn even more about writing, look at Appendix B, "Additional Resources."

Now it's time to reap a return on the money you invested in this book. Here's how: Write a memo asking for a raise. If you can do that, you know the time you've spent with this book has been worth your while. Go ahead, do it. The worst thing that can happen is that your request will be denied. Even if this happens, your writing will have made an impression. If you presented a few good arguments, your supervisor will remember them. Your next raise will probably come sooner as a result. The best thing that can happen, of course, is that you will get a raise. How can you lose? Even if you don't send the memo, write it. It will build your confidence, and maybe you'll send it at a more opportune time. In the meantime, you can think about what you want to say in the memo, revise it, and add to it.

Whenever you have an idea you want to be taken seriously, write a memo. It won't be long before people begin to notice that you can communicate well with written words. The ability to write well is a skill that will help you not only in business, but in many other areas of your life.

APPENDIX A

TWO-WORD VERBS

The English language is full of two-word verbs: verb-preposition combinations that are used in place of a single verb. These can be especially confusing for nonnative speakers. Each sentence below uses a verb-preposition combination. The combinations are highlighted and defined in the parentheses that follow each one. Many writers avoid these combinations, simply because they are confusing, and use the single-word equivalent instead.

The couple **broke up** (separated).
The elevator **broke down** (stopped working) this morning.
They unexpectedly **broke off** (stopped) this relationship.

Competition **brings out** (reveals) his best work.
I hate to **bring up** (raise) such a touchy subject.

Lawrence and Stacy **called off** (canceled) their engagement.
The governor **called up** (summoned) the National Guard.

Please call if anything **comes up** (arises).
Tell us how the game **came out** (ended).

Elizabeth doesn't **care for** (like) green beans.

It won't be long before they **catch up to** (overtake) us.
Tamara **catches on** (learns) quickly.

Doris **filled out** (completed) the application.
Paige **filled up** (filled) the car with gas.
Janet will **fill in** (cover) for me this afternoon.

See if you can **find out** (discover) her birth date.

Billy should **get along** (manage) fine without our help.
Beverly hates to **get up** (arise) in the morning.
Loren **gets away** (goes undiscovered) with everything.
Becky **gets out of** (avoids) work whenever she can.
Get rid of (Discard) this extra lumber.

The losing army finally **gave up** (surrendered).
We don't **give out** (dispense) that kind of information.

The troops will **head out** (leave) in the morning.
Sandy will **head up** (lead) the committee.

I **help out** (assist) whenever I can.

Morris couldn't **hold in** (contain) his disappointment.
The doctors don't **hold out** (promise) much hope.
The strike **held up** (delayed) production.

Don't **leave out** (omit) any of the details.

Gordon will **look into** (examine) this problem.
Doug tried to **look up** (locate) the information.
Older siblings often **look after** (tend, protect) younger ones.
Since the rain, things are **looking up** (improving).

The pilot could barely **make out** (see) the runway lights.
Make out (complete) a grocery list for me.
The thieves **made off with** (took) over two thousand dollars.
The witness **made up** (invented) the story.

Mrs. Henderson is **open to** (considering) your suggestion.
Eventually, the suspect began to **open up** (reveal).

Don't **pass up** (overlook) this opportunity.
The old vicar **passed away** (died).
The singer **passed out** (fainted) from fright.

We expect you to **put forward** (expend) your best effort.
Alex sometimes **puts off** (postpones) his homework.
The boys tried to **put out** (extinguish) the fire.
It's hard to **put up with** (tolerate) incompetence.

Felix **ran across** (discovered) some interesting information.
I'm tired of **running after** (chasing) this ghost of an idea.
These chips will **run out** (be consumed) before we ever start eating.

I think I'll **sit out** (rest) during the next match.

This product should **stand up** (last) under extreme heat.
Why don't you **stand up for** (defend) yourself?

His daughter **takes after** (resembles) him.
Take apart (disassemble) this clock and see why it won't work.

We don't like it when you **talk down** (condescend) to us.

Sam likes to **talk around** (avoid, bypass) the real issue.

Will they **turn down** (reject) our request?
A computer virus can **turn up** (arise) at any time.
I think I'll **turn in** (retire) for the night.

My time and money is all **used up** (consumed).

The wolf **walked into** (entered) the trap.
Don't **walk out** (leave) on us now!

We'll try to **work around** (avoid) the obstacles.
Let's **work out** (resolve) our differences.
I'll **work up** (develop) a proposal for you.
See if the dentist can **work** me **in** (schedule me) this afternoon.

Write down (record) everything you remember from that conversation.
Can you **write in** (include) a clause about late payment?

APPENDIX | B

ADDITIONAL RESOURCES

Using this book is just the first step toward becoming a better writer. If you want to learn more, you can. If you have Internet access, you can use one of the many on-line writing labs. Many high schools and colleges offer inexpensive writing courses for adults in their communities. You may even be able to find a teacher willing to tutor you for a modest fee. If you want to strike out on your own, here is a list of books and websites you'll find helpful and a little information about each one.

Books

1001 Pitfalls in English Grammar (Barron's)

> A problem-solving approach to writing and grammar; very useful for nonnative speakers of English.

Better English by Norman Lewis (Dell)

> Useful for general information; for both native and nonnative speakers of English.

English Made Simple by Arthur Waldhorn and Arthur Ziegler (Made Simple Books)

> Designed for nonnative speakers of English; also good for native speakers with little grammar background.

Errors in English and How to Correct Them by Harry Shaw (Harper-Collins)

> Addresses specific problems in both writing and grammar; useful for nonnative speakers of English.

Grammar by James R. Hurford (Cambridge University Press)

> Thorough coverage of parts of speech, sentence structure, usage, punctuation, and mechanics; especially good for native speakers of English.

The Handbook of Good English by Edward D. Johnson (Washington Square Press)

> A well-organized, comprehensive handbook for both grammar and writing.

Living in English by Betsy J. Blusser (National Textbook Company)

> Specially designed for nonnative speakers of English.

Practice with Idioms by Ronald E. Feare (Oxford University Press)

> For nonnative speakers of English.

Smart English by Anne Francis (Signet)

> A thorough general-purpose handbook for both writing and grammar; good for nonnative speakers of English.

Improve Your Writing for Work by Elizabeth Chesla (LearningExpress)

> Focuses on the larger aspects of writing—stating and supporting your main idea, organizing your thoughts, writing introdutions and conlusions—for workpalce writing such as memos and reports.

Writing Smart by Marcia Lerner (Princeton Review)

> Good for general writing skills; well organized so information is easy to find.

Websites

http://www.english.upenn.edu/~jlynch/grammar

> A comprehensive grammar, style, and mechanics website that explains *everything* briefly and provides links to more in-depth explanations.

http://owl.english.purdue.edu/writing

> A comprehensive on-line writing lab with explanations for every area of writing. Accompanied with workshops and exercises. Many links to other writing-help centers. On-line tutors available.

http://www.umich.edu/gateway/catalog/owl

> An on-line writing lab where you can mail a paper for comments and suggestions.

http://www.ppcc.ccoes.edu/dept/eds/owl

> An on-line writing lab with handouts and on-line writing assistants.

http://www.taft.cc.ca.us/www/tc/tceng/owl.html

> An on-line writing lab with specific help and on-line tutors. Many helpful links.

http://www.rpi.edu/dept/llc/writecenter/web/net-writing.html
> Provides links to best-known and most-used on-line writing labs.

http://www.lang.uiuc.edu/r-li5/esl/
> A comprehensive website for ESL speakers/writers, offering help with organization, writing, punctuation, grammar. On-line writing assistants available.

http://www.aitech.ac.jp/~iteslj/quizzes/
> Self-study quizzes for ESL speakers/writers, covering slang, holidays, reading, culture, writing, grammar, idioms, vocabulary. Helpful links to other websites.

http://babel.uoregon.edu/yamada/guides/esl.html
> A well-indexed guide to websites for ESL speakers/writers.

INDEX

FOUR WAYS
TO PASS ANY CIVIL SERVICE OR JOB-RELATED EXAM...

IT ISN'T LUCK!

Most civil service and job-related exams test you in four major skills: Reading Comprehension, Math, Vocabulary & Spelling, and Writing Skills. ALL of these exams test at least two of these skills. Master these skills and you can pass any civil service or job-related basic skills exam that's given.

What is the best way to prepare?

LearningExpress offers skill-building guides for each of the key areas above. Each is designed to help you learn the important skills you need, in the least amount of time.

Arranged in 20 quick and easy lessons, each manual:

- Pinpoints the areas where you need the most help
- Gives you hundreds of exercises in test format to give you plenty of practice—with full explanations by experts
- Provides you with specific information and tips on how to take a test to score your best
- Helps you increase your skills in just twenty minutes a day

GIVE YOURSELF THE EXCLUSIVE LEARNINGEXPRESS ADVANTAGE!

The LearningExpress exclusive advantage is a necessity! Our unique guides teach the most important basic skills in the least amount of time.

1. ___	**READING COMPREHENSION IN 20 MINUTES A DAY**	Item #039-0
2. ___	**WRITING SKILLS IN 20 MINUTES A DAY**	Item #040-4
3. ___	**VOCABULARY/SPELLING IN 20 MINUTES A DAY**	Item #041-2
4. ___	**PRACTICAL MATH IN 20 MINUTES A DAY**	Item #042-0

SPECIFICATIONS: 8 1/2 × 11 • 176-192 PAGES • $16.00 EACH (PAPERBACK)

TAKING A CIVIL SERVICE OR JOB-RELATED TEST? GO PREPARED!

ORDER THE LEARNINGEXPRESS SKILL BUILDERS YOU NEED TODAY:

Fill in the quantities beside each book and mail your check/money order*
for the amount indicated (please include $6.95 postage/handling
for the first book and $1.00 for each additional book) to:

LearningExpress, Dept. A040, 20 Academy Street, Norwalk, CT 06850

Or call, TOLL-FREE: **1-888-551-JOBS, Dept. A040,** to place a credit card order.

Also available in your local bookstores

Please allow at least 2-4 weeks for delivery. Prices subject to change without notice   *NY, CT, & MD residents add appropriate sales tax

Order Form

CALIFORNIA
____ @ $35.00 CA Police Officer
____ @ $35.00 CA State Police
____ @ $35.00 CA Corrections Officer
____ @ $20.00 CA Law Enforcement Career Guide
____ @ $35.00 CA Firefighter
____ @ $30.00 CA Postal Worker
____ @ $35.00 CA Allied Health

NEW JERSEY
____ @ $35.00 NJ Police Officer
____ @ $35.00 NJ State Police
____ @ $35.00 NJ Corrections Officer
____ @ $20.00 NJ Law Enforcement Career Guide
____ @ $35.00 NJ Firefighter
____ @ $30.00 NJ Postal Worker
____ @ $35.00 NJ Allied Health

TEXAS
____ @ $35.00 TX Police Officer
____ @ $35.00 TX State Police
____ @ $35.00 TX Corrections Officer
____ @ $20.00 TX Law Enforcement Career Guide
____ @ $35.00 TX Firefighter
____ @ $30.00 TX Postal Worker
____ @ $32.50 TX Allied Health

NEW YORK
____ @ $30.00 NYC/Nassau County Police Officer
____ @ $30.00 Suffolk County Police Officer
____ @ $30.00 NY State Police
____ @ $30.00 NY Corrections Officer
____ @ $20.00 NY Law Enforcement Career Guide
____ @ $35.00 NY Firefighter
____ @ $30.00 NY Postal Worker
____ @ $35.00 NY Allied Health

ILLINOIS
____ @ $25.00 Chicago Police Officer
____ @ $30.00 Illinois Allied Health

FLORIDA
____ @ $35.00 FL Police Officer
____ @ $35.00 FL Corrections Officer
____ @ $20.00 FL Law Enforcement Career Guide
____ @ $30.00 FL Postal Worker
____ @ $32.50 FL Allied Health

MASSACHUSETTS
____ @ $30.00 MA Police Officer
____ @ $30.00 MA State Police Exam

The MIDWEST
(Illinois, Indiana, Michigan, Minnesota, Ohio, and Wisconsin)
____ @ $30.00 Midwest Police Officer Exam
____ @ $30.00 Midwest Firefighter Exam

The SOUTH
(Alabama, Arkansas, Georgia, Louisiana, Mississippi, North Carolina, South Carolina, and Virginia)
____ @ $25.00 The South Police Officer Exam
____ @ $25.00 The South Firefighter Exam

NATIONAL EDITIONS
____ @ $14.00 Civil Service Career Starter
____ @ $12.95 Bus Operator Exam National Edition
____ @ $12.95 Sanitation Worker Exam National Edition
____ @ $12.95 U.S. Postal Service 470 Battery Exam
____ @ $14.95 Armed Services Vocational Aptitude Battery

NATIONAL STANDARDS EXAMS
____ @ $20.00 Home Health Aide National Standards Exam
____ @ $20.00 Nurse's Assistant National Standards Exam
____ @ $20.00 EMT-Basic National Standards Exam

To Order, Call TOLL-FREE: 1-888-551-JOBS, Dept. A040

Or, mail this order form with your check or money order* to:
LearningExpress, Dept. A040, 20 Academy Street, Norwalk, CT 0685

Please allow at least 2-4 weeks for delivery. Prices subject to change without notice

LEARNING EXPRESS
An Affiliate Company of Random House, Inc.